What Are You Doing the Rest of Your Life?

Inspiration for Life, Living and Happiness

Jeanene "J C" Childers

What Are You Doing the Rest of Your Life?
Inspiration for Life, Living and Happiness
by Jeanene "J C" Childers

Published by

MileHigh Press

Mile High Press, Ltd.
www.MileHighPress.com
MileHighPress@aol.com
303-885-2207

The Book Shepherd: Judith Briles, Judith@Briles.com
Book Designer: Nick Zelinger, NZGraphics.com

ISBN: 978-1-885331-81-6 (paper)
ISBN: 978-1-0879-7854-3 (POD Indie Pub)
ISBN: 978-1-885331-82-3 (ebook)
LCCN: data on file

Memoir | Inspirational | Communications

First Edition | Printed in the United States

To all the folks I've had the pleasure and joy of calling my friends and with whom I've added marvelous memories and have been the weavers within my life. Each has a made a memory worth remembering and sharing. I would name you all, but at this age (88) and stage, I might accidentally miss one, and would never forgive myself. Hopefully, you remember your part in my life journey we spent together and find it a happy memory, too.

I would be amiss not to name my darling parents who loved each other so much they defied all odds to be together during tough times. Lorraine and Raymond York gave me life, love and inspiration to be the best me I could be.

Just know you've carved your name in my heart and brain and there it will forever remain.

Love you all,

Contents

Author's Note

AS LONG AS I can remember, I've wanted to write a book. I declare everyone has one in 'em! FINALLY ... I've done it on my first attempt!

I have consulted numerous professionals who have had successes with their own books and speaking engagements. If there was a motivational speaker out there, you can bet that I was sitting in his or her audience taking copious notes!

I've always felt I can't make all the mistakes in the world, nor can anyone. There's not enuf time or merit for negatives in life. In creating and completing *What Are You Doing the Rest of Your Life?*, my wish is that it helps others recognize a problem, find a solution, and implement success.

I want others to avoid pitfalls that I've already experienced. After all, I've stepped in the doo doo first—no reason for them to do it, is there?

Did you know that a sixty second negative robs one of a whole MINUTE of a positive? Time is your most precious commodity. Don't WASTE it!

The real secret to my long life that has been filled with happenings and memories is to not give any time and energy to negatives. I learned that POSITIVITY makes life smile from the inside out.

Before my mind rusts and my bones turn to dust, I promised myself that I would create something worth writing and make it worth reading. With the publishing of *What Are You Doing the Rest of Your Life?*, I've done both. I hope you enjoy my journey through my life as much as I did, and do, living it. Make yours even more memorable for others to live by.

Now, I REALLY want to know: "What Are You Doing the Rest of Your Life?" Find me on my website: **www.JCChildersAuthor.com** or email me: *JCrealt@outlook.com.* Write or call, I can't wait to hear from you!

P.S. Look for my next book, *PAWS and SMILE,* about experiences with the "fur children" in your life—the funny/zany experiences they create and the joyous effect they deliver.

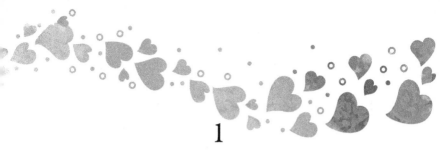

1

Meet My Generation ... The Silent Generation

What's your fondest dream/goal in life?
And most importantly: Why haven't you pursued it?

I'M ONE OF the last members of the "Silent Generation," our numbers are dwindling rapidly. I am fortunate to still be able to remember and share events of the "Great Depression" and growing up as a teenager in World War II, with a favorite uncle serving in the Army. My desire is to share with those who missed the finer points of this era of life. Thus, my book shares my adventures and ahas: *What Are You Doing the Rest of Your Life?* It touches on life in that time—the good, the bad, the ugly and survival of all.

There were so many lessons learned on the battle-field of life by keeping your wits about you, and facing and surviving the challenges presented. Many of my peers of this generation have passed on. Others have lost the ability to tell about it. I'm still here and what you will read; what you will hear from me when you hear me speak will continue with their voices ... and mine.

Alzheimer's, though it's always been there, is now more recognized and personally faced by a three in one ratio. It's kind of scary. One in three will personally face the demons of dementia, while the other two struggle to take care of the afflicted. It's not a pretty picture to paint for future generations. It's a picture of exhaustion, frustration, and expenses—meaning money. Professionals are trying to find a cure—a most difficult task and one quite frustrating. With hope in heart, a portion of my book sales will be donated to Alzheimer's search for the cure. Many friends have suffered as caregivers of loved ones. It's a heartbreaking, difficult task and too frequently the caregiver is lost before the patient because of the stress it causes.

I think I was born with sand in my shoes.

As the caregiver of the man in my life who was lost to diabetes before "Early Onset" dementia claimed him, I sought help through support groups and doctors. There are books available. My favorite that I recommend is *The 36-Hour Day*, available on Amazon and frequently updated with the latest information available. I have learned of another wonderful book for the caregivers of this illness. *My Life Rearranged* by Susan Miller is a great support tome. Add it to your library of "Lifesavers."

Silent Generation members were born in 1925 to 1945. Almost in the middle, I was born in 1932.

I've been very fortunate to have survived a lotta stuff and hope sharing it with you will encourage you to smooth out the bumps that come along in life and keep you trekking. Too many folks give up too soon. Like Auntie Mame proclaimed in the movie of that name, "Life is a banquet and a lot of poor souls are starving to death."

Think about it! What's your fondest dream/goal in life? And most important: Why haven't you pursued it? No time better'n today to shoot for the stars. If you end up in the Milky Way, you're better off than landing in the weeds of despair. What have you got to lose by trying? The world awaits you!

I was born, as were my parents and grandparents, in a friendly little town in the very heart of America— Junction City, Kansas. I'm 4th of eight generations there, with many still happily living the good lives of our forebearers and contributing to the good of all.

I think I was born with "sand in my shoes" ...
curious about what was going on beyond yon hill.
I needed to know if I was missing something and
would set out to find out. My journey of 88 years
has taken me on a fabulous quest. I've had heart-
aches and tribulations, zestful experiences, and
plenty of learning curves. I've met the greatest
people in the world and still call them friends.
A piece of each of them lives in a special room in
my heart and I've gained such joy just knowing
them. To have a friend, one must first be one. The
lowly turtle would never have gotten anywhere
without sticking his neck out.

I've lived abroad eleven years and circled the globe
four times. I was not rewarded with children of my
own in the natural anatomical manner. Oh, but I
have several daughters, sons and grans. And friends
who have shared theirs with me. They have each
added special joy to my personal world. We needed
each other! And always will.

5

When we returned to Germany from years in Thailand and Okinawa, Yvonn came into my life. She was seven when we first met, a little German neighbor girl who came into my life when I painted a life-size Santa on my door in the mountain village of Taunusstein Hahn.

When we returned to the USA, Yvonn's mom brought her to me for a three-month stay to pick up the language. That three months stretched to over a year. She graduated from my old high school; made many lifetime friends; and most importantly, made my mom a grandmother! She's flown Lufthansa as a flight attendant for many years and is now in her 50's. She comes to visit as often as she can and communicates daily via text and email.
My mother loved her German granddaughter! And it was mutual!

Life has been so good to me.

Then, there's my darling "daughter" Jennifer, whose 50th birthday we've just celebrated. She gifted me with two of the cutest, smartest granddaughters the world has beheld. Both graduated with highest honors last year, Madison from college and Hannah from high school. Hannah was added to life by my encouragement. As an only child, I didn't want Madi to lose out on having a sibling, something that I never had. They are BFFs and love each other so much. I have proudly attended all celebrations, including Madi's adorable *Star Wars* themed wedding. She has a great job on the East Coast with her darling man. Both girls were so supportive during Jennifer's bout with cancer and divorce. What a gift to the world and me they are!

And, of course my "Grandson" Adam. He and his mom volunteered to help me clear out a storage room in my home and carry stuff to the Salvation Army. Dad Scott even got involved building a fence with Adam for our shelter dog and my man Stan's walking pal, Blackie. Mom Nancy had Blackie flown from Salt Lake City by "Dog is My Copilot," and we were housing him 'til a home could be found for a 111 pound Border Collie/Great Pyrenees. Blackie was a big fella!

Meanwhile, our last Sheltie passed and Blackie convinced us he was ready to fill the gap. While helping me, Adam asked Nancy if she thought it would be all right to ask me to be his Grandma. Her answer: "Ask her!" In a New York nanosecond, I not only got a wonderful, smart grandson but a darling Bonus Daughter and Bonus Son. And now, a Bonus Dog to live with me. I had been friends of Adam's grandparents before we lost them.

Life has been so good to me. Friends are the best gifts one can give oneself. Don't cut yourself short.

- Life is full of positive happiness if you just open yourself up to it! It's a win-win all the way!

- Life is full of humor if you just seek it, recognize it, and share it with others.

My angel mother used to say, "From the day you ride in a carriage 'til the day you ride in a hearse, there's nothing quite so bad but what it couldn't be worse."

At the end of chapter three onward, I will share a **FOOD for THOUGHT**. Here's my opening:

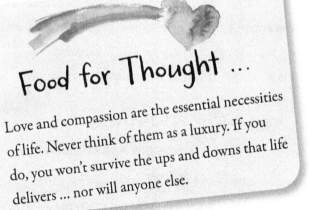

Food for Thought ...

Love and compassion are the essential necessities of life. Never think of them as a luxury. If you do, you won't survive the ups and downs that life delivers ... nor will anyone else.

Enjoy my journey. I have.

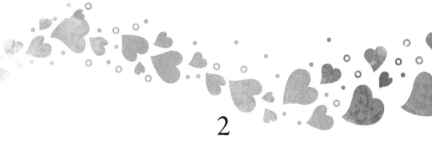

2

My Beginning

If I had known any better, I would have turned around and gone back in.

IT WAS BLIZZARDY cold in Kansas. Besides Niagara Falls freezing over in New York, it seemed the entire world had frozen over. The year? It was 1932, three years into the Great Depression. Headlines continued to shake the world.

Niagara Falls Freezes Over

Great Depression Runs Rampant

Food Lines in Every Village in America

Families Open Doors and Hearts to Needy

And then hope started to surface.

January 16, 1932, was another day of hope. Why? Because I decided it was going to be my Birthday. My mother went into a heavy, painful labor. My father had warmed the Model T and struggled through the snowdrifts and ice to bring my Great Aunt Anne to my mother's bedside to help. I'd already waited two weeks beyond the due date, and she was uncomfortable, to say the least.

The "Great Depression" (whatever in the world was GREAT about it?) should have been called "Horrid! Horrible! Horrendous!" It was causing untold disasters everywhere! Suicides ran rampant by those who'd lost it all, including hope and faith. Feelings across America were of total helplessness. Food lines were without enough to go around. NO jobs. Lack of hope of when there'd ever be any! Total despair!

If I had known any better, I would have turned around and gone back in. After all, Mom was warm, comfortable, and kept me fed. Obviously, I didn't— it wouldn't have been fair to her—and medically, a bit impossible.

The world I was to be born into was in terrible straits! I really didn't want any part of it. But for Mom's sake, I couldn't delay my entrance any longer!

Lorraine was finally going to have her baby!

Communication was extremely limited in the thirties. Cell phones were not invented 'til decades later. The only thing folks had was the "party line" phone hanging on the kitchen wall, which was always busy. Most of the time, everyone spoke to each other at the same time, hence called "party line." TVs did not exist. Radios were listened to in the evening, so the party line was the social network for women in every city.

For my debut, this was a blessing in disguise for once. Grandma anxiously cut into the numerous conversations going on and explained the situation. Lorraine was finally going to have her baby!

The neighbors sprang into action! One farmer warmed his Model T and came for Mom and Pop.

He raced them to the hospital. Another
contacted Dr. Fred O'Donnell to apprise him of
the situation and another went to pick him up
and take him to the hospital. Mom was growing
weaker and losing a lot of blood. The alarms were
sounding. It was looking as if Lorraine and the baby
were not going to make it! The collective "we"
DESPERATELY needed Dr. Fred at once!

In the rush up the hospital outside steps, Dr. Fred
took a hard fall in his race to get to us in time.
Down he went, hurting his leg badly. Dragging
himself up, he continued to reach Mom. She and
I needed help; our lives depended on him! He got
there to save us both, despite his injury and pain.
You saved our lives, Dr. Fred! Thank you! God
Bless you!

Many years later, they built a new hospital in
Junction City and turned the old one into apartments. The steps disappeared.

I returned home after 11 years abroad to be near my parents for their trips over the Rainbow Bridge, their final passage as they took their last breaths.

At the time, we had friends living in one of those apartments where my husband and I frequently played bridge with a couple. Ginger had MS, but never seemed to have any equilibrium problems. She never fell. I, on the other hand, took three tumbles over absolutely nothing. Nothing!

Interestingly, the communities of Fort Riley and Junction City believed that ghosts inhabited many of the apartments and old stone buildings. Word was out that now the ghosts were in the old hospital, now our friends' apartment complex. Ghosts would drop in to visit current residents. Was Dr. Fred's ghost my nemesis because of his fall and my part in it? Three times I shook my fist and said out loud, "Dr. Fred, are you still trying to get even with me for your leg? AND, by the way, wasn't that slap to get me breathing just a bit rougher than it needed to be?"

I was always curious—
6 months.

I loved my Teddy from
Great Aunt Nellie—age 3.

3

Meet Mom and Pop, My Parents

He followed them, far enough behind they never knew he was anywhere near.

MY PARENTS MET during the Roaring '20s. Desperation wasn't in every soul ... yet. Within one year of their marriage, there wasn't enough food to go around. Everyone tightened belts and set extra places at the table and shared everything they had with those who had nothing. The Great Depression was a misnomer. It was really the Awful Depression. Yet, their attitude of gratitude rang supreme as everyone pitched in to help one another survive the dark shadow of the economy.

My father, Raymond, was the area sign painter and grandson of the local Baptist minister. He had been dating the cutest little curly-haired Catholic girl, Lorraine—my mom-to-be. At that time of life, in their small world in Kansas, that was not encouraged! Both families rebelled when it started looking serious. They clucked like old hens: *It would never work!*

Both families suggested they take a "time out'" which they attempted to please their parents. It didn't last long.

Mom loved to dance and had lotsa good-looking beaus taking her dancing. Pop, as a Baptist, was not allowed to dance. You remember the story of Salome, dancing in with John the Baptist's head on a platter. That was serious stuff and Baptists didn't approve of dancing because of that. Too bad! I know Pop would have been a great dancer.

Well, one night, George, a wannabe beau, picked up Mom in his Model T and they headed over to "Whiskey Lake Country Club" where a great ragtime band was playing. When Pop got wind of it, he hopped into his Model T and the pursuit was on. Clever Pop followed them far enough behind so they never knew he was anywhere near. He later claimed to his parents that he was just making sure Lorraine would be all right.

Parking the Model T, he watched them dance from a distance behind a tree. The longer he watched, the angrier he became. When he could take no more, he made a quick getaway; he put the "high speed" Model T into gear and took off. The problem was the takeoff was over the railroad tracks that led into town.

Can't you just hear the sound as he managed to blow out all four tires and drive home on the rims?

Mom and Pop: Lorraine Robinson York
and Raymond Archibald York.

Grandma was in a rage! She accused Raymond of
drinking. Something he NEVER did, following the
Baptist code as he should! Besides, Kansas was dry
'til I was an adult, some twenty-plus years later!
Oh yes, there were bootleggers in Kansas, but Pop
never imbibed. He'd rather spend the little he had

taking pretty Lorraine to the "talkies." Movies were changing, and Lorraine loved them.

Speaking of imbibing, the Attorney General of Kansas took his position and responsibilities seriously. He was so adamant about prohibition in Kansas, he forbade alcohol to be sold in planes flying over the sunflower state. I often wondered how anyone would know or ever enforce that.

She took it seriously.

Mom's very favorite movie was *Lilac Time*, a love story of a pilot who had to fly off to WWI. When he was leaving, he sang his variation of the love song "Jeannine, I Dream of Lilac Time" ...

> *When I return, I'll make you mine.*
> *For you and I, our love dreams will never die,*
> *Jeannine, My Queen of Lilac time.*

21

From which I was named, though Mom spelled it differently.

My parents-to-be had fallen madly in love, despite the admonitions of both families. It was Valentine's Day 1931. Pop gave Mom the prettiest Valentine that he had created straight from his heart. "Be Mine" was written big and bold. She took it seriously. A Justice of the Peace married them that very night. And thus was initiated my lifelong love of hearts and my logo!

Now, they had a problem. Where were they to live?! Alas, there was no room at the parental inn! Mom's Catholic home was full—several of her siblings and their mates already claiming what extra rooms there were. On Pop's side, his sister had recently married and moved to Wyoming with her military husband. The inn was open to both Baptists and Catholics at Grandpa York's farm.

With his painting skills, Pop was able to trade painting signs on grocery store windows for things which the farm did not produce. Grandpa had a cow for milk and a flock of chickens for meat and eggs. They managed the arrangement for several years.

> Grandpa was the loudest
> and the first to complain.

During this time, it was extremely hard for ALL! There were certain stipulations each had to contend with.

The main problem in the household was the lack of understanding and acceptance of each other's beliefs. Grandpa's father was a Baptist minister. At that era, Catholicism was unacceptable by Baptists. Mom and Pop quickly learned that when one was faced with NO choices, one does the best to make whatever's available accepting and agreeable. They all tried very hard to keep everything copacetic!

Though Grandpa never went to church with Grandma Nell, who was there every time the door opened, he forbid anyone living in his house to pass the portal to the Catholic Church. He was the loudest and the first to complain if anyone got near the Catholic church. It wasn't until we left the farm that Mom could return to her faith without conflict. I'm so happy the World's become more tolerant and compassionate. There are still some factions that differ and insist upon *their* way. It's so much better to understand and love rather than hate!

When I started school, I was encouraged to make my own decision about my faith. My little girlfriends and I attended every church in town. No door was closed to us. We wanted to see firsthand what and how they believed; what and how they worshiped and did so our entire youth. It gave us a broad view of religion. Several of us even became Sunday School teachers.

Food for Thought ...

It's a valuable lesson in many ways. Throughout life, I've continued to learn all I can about ALL religions and keep an open mind and respect for each. I studied them all and as an adult chose to follow in my mother's footsteps. I felt "at home" with the rituals of Catholicism, while accepting choices of others. Too much of it is too human-inspired. The prime importance of any faith is to believe in something greater than oneself. And, at the same time, keep an open mind and follow your heart.

4

"Paint" ... My Pony
for a Day

1940

There was no other word for it ... Pop was livid!

GRANDMA YORK'S BABY brother had a horse
stable and, in his livery, he had a pretty pony named
"Paint." I don't know how he did it, but he convinced his sister Nellie that I needed to have that
pony. Not only did she buy him for me, she bought
a beautiful pair of red jodhpurs and insisted I wear
them when she took me to town to show me the
"surprise" awaiting me there.

My beloved pony for a day—Paint.

Oh, how excited I was when I mounted Paint! My very own pony! It was love at first sight! BUT I'd barely had my picture taken on him at the stable when Pop arrived on the scene. There was no other word for it ... Pop was livid! Pop was extremely overprotective of his single chick and would NOT

hear of my owning anything that big that could
move on its own.

> *You could fall off and break a leg.*
> *The pony could gallop out of control and you*
> *would fly off.*
> *You will fall off and hit your head and have*
> *a concussion.*

On and on the negatives mounted 'til Grandma
threw up her hands and gave up, returning Paint to
great Uncle Archie. I was so upset. No amount
of crying could persuade him that Paint and I
belonged together.

Before owning his livery, Uncle Archie had been a
Pony Express rider, carrying mail on a fast horse.
Little did he know what a short career that would
be. Within less than a year, the railroads came in
and mail had a faster way to reach its readers.
Uncle Archie was issued an 1861 cap and ball
Colt Revolver to protect himself from Indians
and wild animals.

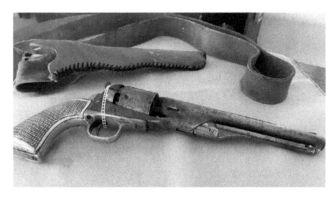

Great Uncle Archie's cap and ball Colt revolver that always
rode with him on the Pony Express trail in 1861.

Today, I'm the proud owner of that pistol! I have
taken it to antique road shows in South Dakota and
Colorado. Appraisers were quite impressed with its
matching numbers on each part of the
gun. The carved ivory handle is beautiful, and its
condition is excellent. However, they had difficulty
giving it similar evaluations. It seems the Colt
Factory had a fire that destroyed records for that
particular model. I still have it with its leather
holster.

Though monetary value was questionable, it's worth a great deal to this Pony Express great niece.

Food for Thought ...

Two things define you: patience when you have nothing and attitude when you have everything.

5

Growing Up in a World at War

1941

Rarely were women recognized at that time for their contributions.

AS IF GROWING up in a depression, poor as "Church Mice" and doing without, were not enough, 7 December 1941, gave our world an even greater challenge—World War II!

The Japanese bombed Pearl Harbor and changed our lives in many more ways. War was declared! Every able bodied man was drafted to serve. Wars do provide jobs for many who had none before, but robbed society of the strongest men and willing patriots. The draft went into effect, culling the young and healthy men from society. Those who had certain physical detriments were considered "4F," unsuitable for service, and stayed on the American shores to build ships and planes and tanks.

For a nine year old, it was scary when Pop and my mother's two brothers headed out the door together. Their destination: the enlistment center! I had no idea what an enlistment center was. All I knew, I felt, was that Mom wasn't excited about their leaving together. Of the three of them, only my Uncle Lloyd was accepted. Family men were excused from the draft as they were needed to provide for their families.

When they ran short of men for these tasks, an army of Rosie the Riveters took over in factories and wherever they could be of help. Great Aunt Anne, who came to Mom's aid, was an Army nurse in Hawaii. Women pilots became stealth pilots, joining the Army Air Corps flying planes where they were needed in other parts of the world so the "men" could fly them into combat as well as used for cargo drops. Rarely were women recognized at that time for their contributions.

It wasn't until decades later that they were formally recognized for their service in air transport and countless other services until the renovation of the hemicycle at the entrance to the Arlington Cemetery which was morphed into the FIRST Memorial to women who served in the Military Services: the Women in Military Services Memorial, also known as WIMSA. The hemicycle was ready for a facelift. Its structure was created on January 16, 1932—the day I was born!

The memorial was dedicated in 1999 and can be viewed and experienced at the entrance to Arlington Cemetery. I was there at the dedication and won a

recognition prize for record ticket sales for the
Million Dollar House donated by a builder in
Washington, DC, in honor of the women who
served. My prize was awarded to me by the current
Wonder Woman herself. It was an all-expense paid
trip for two to Puerto Vallarta, Mexico. I took my
girlfriend, Marie, who was getting a multiple
sclerosis medical retirement from civil service.

Women in our armed services.

I was privileged to personally meet many of the
women who were honored. At the dedication, they
crossed over Memorial Bridge with lighted candles

raised on high. Those who could no longer walk, were pushed in wheelchairs by Girl Scouts. What a sight this must have been from planes coming and going to Ronald Reagan Airport! Although not military, I had a part in the accomplishment and walked proudly across with our lady heroes.

Ceilings of the old structure were replaced with glass on which were etched memorable thoughts. Computers await entry of data of those who have won the right to be recognized. Go visit it! It's quite interesting! Many beautiful memorials have graced the lawns and shores of Washington, DC, but THIS is the FIRST to commemorate women in our country's military services. Oh, such stories they had to share! I have offered to write a book on that. The world needs to know these heroines!

Rationing of all sorts went into effect to provide the materials to build and maintain things needed for the war effort. Personal vehicles within the states were raised onto pillars to protect the tires which could not be replaced. There was little gas available and tightly rationed. Even though combat was not within the United States, we all felt what was going on.

We were trained to frugality— once again.

EVERYTHING WAS RATIONED! Cars, tires, gas, tin cans and rubber. Even shoes were rationed. We didn't drive anywhere that our feet could take us. We walked everywhere.

Anything that was a product used in the war effort was in extremely limited supply. War needs were first and foremost. We were used to doing without during the depression. The Great Depression that we had come out of had become a good training ground for what we now faced. We were trained to frugality—once again.

Do you remember margarine? During the war, white oleomargarine was sold in plastic bags with yellow buttons of food coloring. My kitchen job was to break the yellow button and massage it into the oleo until it resembled butter. It may have looked like butter, but it sure didn't taste like it!

Fortunately, our needs were few in our small town. The cupboards were quite bare with sugar, canned goods, meats and butter limited to the number in the family, ages of the members and physical needs. Beans and rice became the core of every meal! A day didn't go by when I didn't hear these words flow in a singsong from Mom's lips:

> *Beans, beans ... the musical fruit.*
> *The more you eat ... the more you toot!*
> *The more you toot ... the better you feel.*
> *So, let's have beans for every meal!*

Moms were amazing. They birthed the most creative combinations and interesting recipes during this period.

We lived through it and learned a lesson never to be forgotten. Today, I find I still wear my clothes longer; buy only what's absolutely needed and share what others might use. I still shop at thrift stores; and wear clothes out. As Mom always preached: "Willful waste makes woeful want!"

Food for Thought ...

Live honestly. Love generously. Speak kindly. And leave the rest to God.

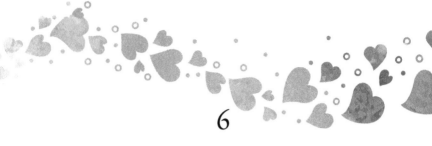

6

Pop's Cars and Teaching Me to Drive at Age 12

1944

I was embarrassed by that old car coming to get me on rainy days.

MY FATHER WAS in high demand in Kansas. As "the local renowned sign painter and artist," calls came in for his services at all times of the day and night. His specialty was gold leaf designs—something that every bank and storefront wanted on their windows during those years.

Pop was also an outdoorsman with a soul and compassion. He killed only what our family could eat and provided us with wild game and fish during the depression and war rationing. He was keen to watch for the fresh green watercress in the clear streams and gather the morel mushrooms in the spring. Mother was a gourmet preparer of all he brought and shared her skills with all. Her squirrel and gravy dish was not to be missed! We ate regularly where so many struggled to fill their bellies.

A few times when I questioned the authenticity of the new and untried, Pop would offer me a nickel "just to taste it." Many became my faves. I learned to appreciate everything they presented to me. Pop also had a love of old cars, especially Model Ts. He would meet farmers who had tucked their cars away during the war and now wanted the newer models. Besides, not everyone could remake an engine or convert the hand crank start (a device not well loved—it broke a lot of arms) to the button starter that was initiated where the heel of the foot would rest.

Pop used to say, "Anyone can buy a new car."

He would always have one "T" running well and three or more under renovation. He knew what he was doing and loved working on them. Routinely, he was approached by others to sell his vehicles to them. It was always a "no." He clung to them like children. He was dedicated to the earlier Fords. Mom, on the other hand, had a Studebaker.

Enter me. As an elementary student, I was embarrassed by that old car coming to get me on rainy days. I would hide behind trees 'til Pop gave up and drove on home. I've been ashamed of that "false pride" many times since. Like Pop used to say, "Anyone can buy new car, but very few have the opportunity to ride in a vintage Model T."

My embarrassment receded by the time I was 12, begging Pop to teach me to drive. He had the 1923 Touring parked off street on a wee bit of land where I was taught the basics that included the skill of being able to move it back and forth about 20 feet each way.

Oh, let me tell you—I ached to get my license and REALLY drive. When that day arrived, I loaded it up with my closest friends and we took a spin over the roller-coaster roads west of town. I chanced to look back at the hill behind to see Pop, following close enough to make sure we were all right, but not so close it disturbed me. Hmmm, now that I think of it—it was much like his checking Mom out when she went dancin' with that other feller so many years before.

I brought "Lizzie" to Parker, Colorado, in 2005, when I sponsored one of our Junction City High School class reunions. I helped with many of the

43

class reunions in Palm Springs, California, Pagosa Springs, Colorado; and J C, of course. By this time, we were scattered all over the United States—so why not have a reunion in different locations?

Eventually, I worked the 2005 Reunion around Parker Days in Parker, Colorado, where I now live. My "Tin Lizzie" was loaded with as many classmates as she could hold and covered with giant sunflowers. Lizzie was the star of the event and won the Judges Favorite prize at Parker Days!

Lizzie is still running, being the "star" in many parades.

Those giant sunflowers were given to attendees at the next class reunion in Pagosa Springs, Colorado.

Food for Thought ...

If there is one thing I've learned, it's best summarized in the words of Eleanor Roosevelt: Life is meant to be lived. That's all there is to it!

7

I Can't Give You Anything But Love, Baby!

1944

We didn't complain; we never got a raise;
and we both dove into the box of
cherry chocolates we got at Christmas.

DO YOU REMEMBER that old song "I Can't Give You Anything But Love, Baby?" Well, that pretty much spells out how life of a preteen was during the Great—I'm still wondering 80 years later what was so great about it!—Depression. They should have used the more descriptive "horrid," "horrendous," "devastating," or even God awful! Few of our classmates had parents and grandparents prepared to spend money on extras for their kids or grandkids.

My best friends and I were lacking everything. There were things others had and we just had to accept we were denied those things or would never have. A new pair of shoes? Not for me, or for them. A store-bought dress instead of the ones Mom made from flour sacks or hand-me-downs from Cousin Phyllis. The flour sacks would just have to do.

My fashion began with two ingredients: my mother's nimble fingers and the store's flour sacks.

For 12 year olds, my chum Corky and I wanted more. Our folks did their best providing us with a roof over our heads and lots of mac and cheese in our tummies. But we wanted a lot MORE! A movie would be the best for us girls, or even a cold soda that would be sipped. And then there was the popcorn—a heavenly splurge—if only we girls could figure out how to get the few coins to satisfy our wishes.

We would make money. We would have movies, sodas, popcorn and no more flour sack dresses!

We respected Pop's advice and understanding. He also had an answer— decided we needed jobs! Corky and I sought out Pop ... my dear daddy who knew everyone in Junction City. He'd have an answer to our need! We weren't afraid of work and were willing to do anything legal and ethical.

We grew up in an Army town. Fort Riley was just next door. Surely someone would want to hire us, and Pop would know who.

Pop, while having coffee with other businessmen, heard them talking about the wives of the young soldiers being sent home to their families while their husbands were deployed abroad. The merchants were losing sales staff and didn't know what to do. Pop suggested that he introduce us to one of the managers of the stores to see if two preteens could fill a couple of the spots. True to his word, he made an appointment with one for an interview and took us to meet Mr. Lambert of Scotts 5 & 10. Before he arrived, he advised us on how to answer questions we were asked and how we should act at our very first-ever interview for a job.

We must have impressed Mr. Lambert. Either that or he was desperate for help. He told us to come back the next day, wearing work clothes appropriate for sweeping the basement stone floors. We were ecstatic! We had jobs! We would make money. We would have movies, sodas, popcorn and no more flour sack dresses!

We arrived at the time he set and were instructed as to how he wanted the stone floors swept.

Merchandise was stored on shelves in the basement. Corky and I had to carefully sweep without causing dust to rise and muss up the merchandise. We set about our task industriously. Try as we might, those rough surfaced stones did not adapt to the method we had chosen to perform our task!

When Mr. Lambert came down to see how we were doing, he could not see us amidst the cloud of dust in the air and everywhere. We were FIRED AND SENT HOME! Dirty tears were running through the dust on our faces. First day! First job ... that had lasted two hours! And we got fired for trying too hard to get the "job" done fast and ignoring and not following Mr. Lambert's instructions! Immediately, we headed for Pop, who was entirely sympathetic with both us AND MR. LAMBERT! Yes, we were guilty of not following instructions and tried really hard to perform the task given to quickly. "We REALLY want this job, Daddy! What can we do?"

"Are you willing to go back to Mr. Lambert with your tails between your legs; apologize from your heart; offer to correct your mistake by sweeping just as he instructs you too; dust all the shelves and merchandise; and do it for FREE ... starting right now?"

"Oh yes, Daddy, if he'll just give us another chance."

Never had that old stone basement floor been cleaner.

"Are you willing to go back down with me right now—before supper? Tell him you are both sorry you didn't follow his instructions to the letter. You were just trying so hard to do a good job and sort of got carried away. You'll make it all right and you'll also dust all the merchandise on the shelves as well, and do all that regardless of how long it takes?"

"Oh yes, yes we will!"

We jumped into Pop's Model T Ford and headed back to Scotts 5 & 10. Mr. Lambert took one look at our now mud-stained faces and listened with his heart to our sorrowful pleas and directed us to come back the next day, which was Saturday, and prove what we offered.

Never had that old stone basement floor been cleaner, and the merchandise survived the test of dust storm that we had created by the end of that Saturday. Mr. Lambert and my father agreed that they had given us one of the harshest lessons we'd ever learn, but one that would make a positive mark on our future lives—and it did. After our cleanup experience, we were promptly rehired. We worked after school and twelve hours on Saturdays until we graduated from high school for a hearty 25 cents an hour. We didn't complain; we never got a raise; and we both dove into the box of cherry chocolates we got at Christmas that just happened to cost 25 cents a box.

Thinking back, I know this decision and action must have been as hard on Pop and Mr. Lambert as it was on Corky and me. But I also know it was an important lesson, well-learned that would long be remembered and valued the rest of our lives.

I have no idea what Corky did with her "fortune." I was very frugal, saving most of those quarters to pay my first year's tuition to Kansas State College, now Kansas State University. We did find time to squeeze in an occasion movie, but never on a

Saturday—we both were in the store from nine in the morning until closing at nine at night.

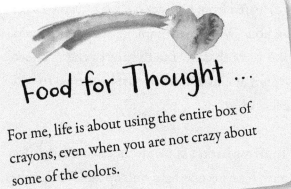

Food for Thought ...

For me, life is about using the entire box of crayons, even when you are not crazy about some of the colors.

8

Uncle Sam Adopts Me

1951

If it is to be, it is up to me.

THOUGH MY HOMETOWN was less than 25 miles from the college, I had no means of transportation to allow commuting from home, nor affordable place to stay. I learned there were "unorganized" houses, privately owned that were reasonable. Eight girls shared the four bedrooms, small living room and kitchen. We named it "Cherie Amie," meaning *good friends*, and I was elected president of *Cherie Amie*.

I found a bookkeeping job with the temporary Student Union, in a temporary building on the future parking lot of the proposed future Student Union, which provided me enough money to pay the meager rent and buy groceries. My roomie, Lillian McGill, was a dear friend and classmate from first grade, whose mother was our second-grade teacher and my all-time fave. Both house and job were a brisk walk from classes and kept me in shape physically and financially. Where there's a will—there's a way. I was determined to go to college. My parents and many of my classmates hadn't been able to because of the Great Depression or World War I or II. So many were robbed of opportunities.

Eventually, the parking lot at Kansas State College morphed into a fine Student Union. The Ag College became a University. My bookkeeping salary covered my share of the rent at *Cherie Amie.*

The choice was good.

It took all my quarters and extra earnings to cover the expenses for what was to be my one year of college. There was NO ONE to help me finance another year or go to nursing school. I had yearned to become a nurse. I applied for a civil service job at Fort Riley, hoping I could work through the summer to pay for future education. In the process, I applied for every possible position in May. The only thing offered was Clerk Typist, GS-3, which was not available until mid-August—too late to help with my plan!

In the meanwhile, I had been working at Cole's Department Store since school was out to save as much as I could. I had few, if any, choices. Civil service paid more, had retirement, health benefits and for the first time in my life "paid vacations!" Without further education this appeared to be my only option. The choice was good. It provided me with opportunities for employment nearly everywhere I went and retirement from the Office of the Secretary of Defense at the Pentagon eventually. Thank you, Uncle Sam!

Food for Thought...

Today's current generations tend to take all that for granted. I was very young when I learned the 10 two-letter words that can make or break a spirit: *If it is to be, it is up to me.*

9

Freedom Is a Wonderful Thing

1954

*If the bird dropped dead, one was instructed
to grab the mask and "get outta Dodge!"*

IT'S NOT EASY being an only child! I always met
barriers when I tried to spread my wings and leave
the nest. Every time I would stick my toe in the
water that I wanted to live on my own, really live
on my own, my parents would let their faces drop
and almost hang their heads. Somehow they took
the mistaken attitude that "I didn't love them
anymore." The furthest thing from the truth.
One NEVER stops loving parents like mine!

59

It was just that I wanted to find out who and what
I was and what was in store for my future. The
world was waiting for my debut. My cousin Betty
had moved to Colorado years ago after college.
I thought she had it all. She skied, traveled, met
interesting people; did fascinating things like
camping and hiking in the Rockies ... and she did
them all when she wanted and how she wanted to.
I was quite stymied in Junction City, Kansas.

Then my angel appeared! And she had wings—big
ones—those of a Frontier Stewardess. Yes, this was
the name given back then.

I was free!

My dear friend and classmate Marilyn (known as
Lynn to all) was back in Junction City for a visit
with her family and came over to visit. My folks

loved her, and when she suggested that I move to Colorado and live with her, I was ready to jump at the opportunity. At long last, I was able to leave home with no hard feelings! My parents accepted that this was an ideal situation saying, "Lynn is such a good and trustworthy friend."

Lynn had opened the door to freedom for me to escape. By getting into the civil service at Fort Riley, I had the option to transfer to other civil service positions throughout the world. My final stop was working at the Pentagon from which I retired after a very long break and other positions. I interviewed for all jobs the Denver area had to offer and chose the one available the soonest.

It didn't take long to realize why my position was so readily available at the Rocky Mountain Arsenal in Colorado. Uncle Sam had chosen to use the 32,000 acres of barren, desolate land to bury dangerous chemical waste. Each employee was issued a gas

mask and a live bird in a cage beside his or her desk.
If the bird dropped dead, one was instructed to grab
the mask and "get outta Dodge!"

I soon transferred to Guided Missile school at
Lowry AFB.

Usually the last one in got the
middle of the double bed.

Lynn's offer of "plenty of room for one more" was
true up to a point—if one were young, adventurous
and flexible. You see, it was a two-bedroom, one
bath unit, housing four stewardesses, an interior
decorator and me. Stews often overnighted at their
destinations in those days so it wasn't as snug as it
could have been.

When everyone was home, it was first in, first choice. And always a game in order of arrival. Twin beds were prime. The double bed in the other bedroom sometimes slept three, sleeping crosswise. Usually the last one in got the middle of the double bed. The curved sectional in the living room was not too bad. We were young; got along quite well with each other; found accommodations affordable and workable. And I was free! Also, on the plus side: stewardesses were frequently overnighting at their destinations.

In my new Guided Missile School office at Lowry Air Force Base, cupid guided a missile and Johnny Bordenave and I fell in love. We married that New Year's Eve. His family came down from Minnesota for the lovely formal church wedding in my hometown, Junction City, KS. I was so naïve that I thought that would assure New Year's Eve dates the rest of my life. But wait, there's more!

Food for Thought ...

Don't carry your mistakes around. Instead, place them under your feet to use as stepping stones for your next adventure.

10

Five Minnesota Winters

1955

I didn't realize that a one-way train ticket to Kansas was the beginning of life once again.

ST. PAUL, MINNESOTA, called to us. When Johnny finished his required three years in the military, we moved to the frigid winters that St. Paul offered. It's a good thing that I had my marriage to keep me warm during those cold winter nights. His folks tried to convince him to find a job for a year or two. Johnny felt differently— he wanted to get his education first and not take night classes and save for his education.

Johnny and I were proud and determined that WE COULD DO IT! After all, it was for "our future!"

Despite their advice, he enrolled in the university. They were not keen about financing his education. Though they were more than able—they chose not to!

My path took me to the Corps of Engineers which was in the post office—two bus rides each way. If I was lucky, I wasn't stuck in the freezing refrigerator cold waiting between. The Corps dredged the bottom of the St. Lawrence Seaway so that boats could get through. Johnny didn't have to deal with the cold the way I did. He drove to and from school in a warm car. We all had goals to achieve and did what we had to do to get there!

I was lucky to have one of those wonders—a wringer washing machine!

Minnesota has the most God-awful winters! Snow from the first snowfall is still on the ground when fresh snow falls atop. By January, to ease midwinter blues, St. Paul sponsors a "Vulcans Winter Fest" with an ice palace and parades ... it celebrates its Scandinavian influence. Chimney sweeps, with faces covered with soot, jump in and out of the parade to smudge and kiss the girls. If you've been smudged by a Vulcan, you'll have very good luck throughout the year. Trust me ... you didn't have to "line up" to receive a smudge kiss—they came right after you!

I lived there five bitterly COLD winters—FIVE of them!

Laundry was always a challenge. I was lucky to have one of those wonders—a wringer washing machine ... meaning that there were quasi paddles to rotate the clothes in the wash tub, then each piece was fed one by one into the wringer that was electric—a true help for housewives at that time. Without a dryer, I had to hang the washed clothes outside to dry. Meaning, they FROZE and had to be hauled to our upstairs apartment to spread out to dry. Oh, how my arthritic hands suffered! One Christmas, Johnny bought me a dryer—no more stiff, frozen laundry!

Every day was a challenge! Pop had trapped the wild Kansas beavers to free up the dammed streams of farmer friends. He sent the tanned hides with me to Denver to have a warm coat made for Mom. She loved it! Now living in Minnesota, Mom sent me her full length beaver coat to ward off the cold. Winds blew right through it! Something HAD to give!

An additional job was offered at the Corps. I could work it in with my current job and all it entailed. I took it! My first goal was to save up enough money to buy a clunker to take me to and from work—no more standing in the "delights" of the Minnesota winter and being subject to a bus schedule. I had accumulated enough money to now shop for some inexpensive transportation. Then I learned a very powerful lesson. Need I say: via the hard way, as usual.

My most painful lesson to date was about to emerge. Couples should have separate bank accounts. And, they should really know whom they can trust. Little did I suspect that the person that I was closest to would betray me. Johnny had withdrawn my funds saved for a car ... to take flying lessons! I had no idea that he was taking them. He never said a peep. And there were other things that I never heard a peep about either. This feller I'd already frozen my buns off for his education funds could do this to me! To this day, I still cannot believe his chutzpah.

I had so wanted to have a child and was deeply dismayed when the doctors finally said it wasn't to be. It wasn't 'til graduation and his securing a job with IBM that his other surprise surfaced. I was informed that his girlfriend was pregnant, and he wanted a divorce ... and he wanted the dryer to dry his baby's diapers. SAY WHAT?!

Learning recently that the child I so longed for wasn't to be was not pain enough. Now, the scoundrel wanted a divorce. When I begged him to stay with me and not get a divorce, in my desperation, I suggested that "we" adopt the baby. "No" was his response. I want her and the baby—not you."

I cried for a YEAR, but not when anyone could see.

After five years of putting him through college, and helping him get a nice job with IBM, the only thing

I was given was ONE share of IBM and a train ticket home to Kansas. Or so I thought.

What I didn't realize was that one-way train ticket to Kansas was the beginning of life once again.

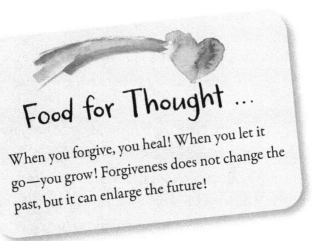

Food for Thought ...

When you forgive, you heal! When you let it go—you grow! Forgiveness does not change the past, but it can enlarge the future!

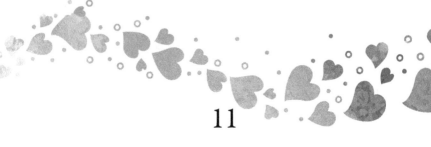

11

Junction City to Colorado to Europe

1960-1961

*Sometimes one leans too hard on others for too long
and it almost breaks everyone and everything.*

UNCLE LEE NEEDED help! My aunt had just
died of cancer and my uncle was besought with
pain. They had two adopted children, now teen-
agers. I stayed with them for the better part of a
year, cooking and cleaning and trying to help as
best I could. The teens were totally incorrigible
and could have cared less about anything I did.
Uncle Lee did NOTHING to help the situation!
He just sat there feeling very sorry for himself.

I felt his pain, was compassionate to their needs, but enough is enough! My mother, his sister, told him to get a grip! God helps those who help themselves! From experience, I knew that Mom was always right.

Uncle Lee owned a thriving locker plant and a farmers' produce business that his brother was keeping alive for him. He finally realized he had become too dependent on the sympathies of those who cared. I think it was an awakening for him. Sometimes one leans too hard on others for too long and it almost breaks everyone and everything. Tough love comes into play!

For the second time, I headed to Denver and Lowry Air Force Base. There was a job waiting for me in the hangar, now known as the Wings Over the Rockies Museum. I compromised my hearing with the jets on the runway, but I regained my life and sense of being.

Across the street was the origination of the US Air Force Academy now a grand complex in Colorado Springs. Young cadets marched to the beat, became officers and went to work for Uncle Sam as I did.

This is when Lynn Parsons came into my life. Her aunt worked in my office. Lynn had just been hired as a French teacher at the local high school and was looking for a roommate. When we met, we instantly became friends and rented a larger apartment. After a while, we decided that if we had two more roomies, we could get a place with a pool and exercise equipment. That would be heaven for us girls.

We went through numerous roomies before two Canadians, Arlene and Margot, showed up and joined us. They were on the first leg of their journey around the world. Arlene's mother had married a pilot and added five more kids to their family. Both stayed with them until they found it a bit too crowded. Then they saw our ad in the paper and applied immediately. When we all met, Lynn and I knew "they were the ones." We got along very well.

All four of us had desires to see the world. We moved again into a less expensive apartment and started saving for our world trip. Each took "second jobs;" moved to a third floor walk-up and gave up the pool. And we started planning for our next adventure.

It was bon voyage time!

Arlene had many beaus, one who decided he was going to marry her. She told him of our plans to see the world and that she'd never get married until she had made that dream come true. After some time, he offered loaning her the money to go to Europe with one condition: when she returned, she would either pay him back ... or marry him. After two weeks conjugating on it, she decided that was her only chance.

I had been in a car accident on 6th Avenue that was caused by the other driver. Her insurance paid my medical bills, replaced my totaled car, and left me enough to travel one way to Europe. One of the officers in my hangar had a friend working for the US military in Frankfurt, Germany. I was offered a job when I arrived there.

Arlene and I accelerated our travel plans. Lynn and Margot would follow the next summer. It was bon voyage time! Arlene and I set sail 15 June 1962, to explore Europe. We drove her car to the port in Montreal, Canada, boarded a passenger vessel, and waved "goodbye" to the mainland. We had the cheapest berth on the ship—right next to the boiler room. We figured we'd arrive in Cobh, Ireland, the same time as the first class passengers and still have enough jingle in our jeans to procure a motorcycle that would seat two to see the British Isles.

One night, Arlene decided to be a bit daring. The first-class section was having a party with a theme: we had to dress like our favorite song. Why I took a muu muu to Europe, I have no idea. But it came in handy and we went to the party. I tied a pillow around my middle, covered it with the muu muu and wore a sign: *I should have danced all night!* I, and it, was a hit.

During our voyage, we became acquainted with an Irish lass aboard ship who advised us: just store your luggage and buy rucksacks. Set off by using our thumbs. Hitchhiking was keen and safe in 1962, I might add. We met the village folks everywhere, who welcomed us into their homes and hearts. There's something about the Irish! The Lorie drivers were most gracious picking us up and giving us free rides. We also were able to hear stories and lore—perhaps that's why they call the trucks "lories"?—about their homeland and history.

Some of the Irish and Scottish invited us to share their homes and pubs. We led the singing in several of the latter. We joined the "Oiges" Youth Hostel in Ireland, where we could stay for fifty cents a night and a "duty," such as cleaning the latrine or other chores. We used them wherever we didn't have other accommodations. Cheap and a terrific way to meet the "real people."

No prearranged three months travel for us.

We learned to do the Highland Fling in the Inverness Castle, reincarnated to a youth hostel. And we joined the "Orangemen's Walk" in Glasgow, staying the night in a couple's home. Their son had just married, and the parents decided they liked these two crazy American gals. They even poured us baths in front of the fireplace. Imagine having to lug tub and water to warmth for bathing. We were ever so grateful! We stayed in B&B's, youth hostels, and traveled with a paperback *Europe on $5 a Day* in our backpack beating the price many times! For Arlene and me, it was more like $2 a day! Sometimes we even slept in the little Renault, when nothing was available.

Dean, Arlene's generous Beau, had arranged for the Renault to be picked up in Paris. It carried us through the continent and opened even greater choices. When we got up each day, we'd flip a coin to see where we should head next. From Paris to Norway, via Holland, Denmark and Sweden, then the Riviera from Norway, where it would be warm and sunny. No prearranged three months travel for us.

Being in Paris on Bastille Day was not the greatest choice of places to be. After having fireworks tossed on us at a sidewalk café, our car transported us South to the Riviera and Montpellier, far from the mad Parisians.

We found and joined a group of Country Folks celebrating the "French 4th of July." They shared their tubes to swirl about in the clean, cool river. Arlene had grown up in an area of Canada where the French language vied for English. She could speak enough of the dialect of Southern France to make us welcome. Then we were invited to join them for a picnic. We quickly discovered that it was a delightful experience! We almost stayed there, but we had so much more to discover. After bidding our new friends goodbye, we checked out Nice, Cannes, Monte Carlo and then pointed the little Renault toward Italy.

Florence is a real living museum as is Rome. The
Ponte Vecchio Bridge was an amazing collection
from art to clothing and everything in between.
We checked out Michelangelo's David, and all the
art we could absorb in one day. We asked where
the natives dined and then headed to one of the
suggested spots to enjoy a sumptuous Italian dinner.

We purchased a gallon bottle of Valpolicella wine
for fifty cents and headed back to our B&B. Then
we climbed out onto the roof from our room with
our bargain treasure. Views of the village from our
vantage point were magnificent. The delightful
bonus was that we had live music from the streets.
Yes, we chose our location well and were happy!

The next day we climbed the Leaning Tower of Pisa
and felt as if we were walking in a leaning position
for hours afterward. NOTE: the tower is again
open since 2001 to limited numbers. It took 11
years—will it hold up 'for 300 more!? Afterward,

we felt as if we were walking in a leaning position for hours. We explored museums, churches and anything recommended. Rather than return to our B&B in Florence, we decided to drive all night into Venice that was next on our list.

It didn't take us as long as we anticipated, and we arrived to water streets and little lighting in the middle of the night. What to do? Tired from the drive, we knew we MUST seek a place to lay our weary heads. Very little was open at the hour we rolled in and we were a bit leery of finding a place to park and sleep in the car.

Little did we know how EARLY those little buggers chose to rise and gallop over our heads!

As we were rolling through the dry part of Venice, we spotted a campground. The office lights were on.

A nice proprietor answered our tap on the door and invited us in. Alas, he had no accommodation and knew of no one who might.

"We do have a boat hull in the center of the park that has benches one could sleep on within ... and a door that locks," he offered shaking his head.

"We'll take it! We have hostel sheets and are totally desperate!"

"Well, if you want it, it's yours. Here's the key. I must tell you, though, the little children take great delight climbing onto the decks to play."

"We won't mind. Thank you and good night!"

Little did we know how EARLY those little buggers chose to rise and gallop over our heads! We made do! Just like brushing our teeth with Valpolicella wine because we'd heard you CAN'T drink the water in Italy! Let me tell you, if you've never brushed your teeth with Valpolicella wine, I do not advise it! It clumps something fierce and is hard to spit out. Besides, it's a frightful waste of good Italian wine!

I was down to $20 in my jeans; hadn't seen anyone about the job which was offered yet; and Arlene, who had decided she had no way to ever pay Dean back, was going to marry him upon returning to Colorado. We headed to Frankfurt, Germany's Auld Sachsenhausen Hostel, and our last fifty cent hostel together.

Food for Thought ...

I just woke up from a dream where everything was possible, and I could achieve anything I wanted to ... then I realized ... I was never asleep!

12

Employment Hoped for ...
to Be Or Not to Be?

1962

Desperation filled my heart as never before!

EARLY THE NEXT morning, Arlene loaded the car up, hit American Express for the money Dean had sent for her to choose a diamond in Holland, then she was on her way to board the ship back home. She smuggled the diamond through customs in a ball of yarn to avoid any fees.

I was dressed as smartly as I could put myself together and headed off to Gruenberg Park in Frankfurt where my promised job existed. When

I got there, I was informed by the colonel that he had to fire someone and could not hire anyone for two months or more. So sorry, but if I could just hang in there for a couple of months ...! The promised job was a now a nonexistent job.

OMG! WhatamIgonnadonow! I was really counting on that job. I need that job. At this point, I only had $20 in my pocket. Living in the youth hostel at 50 cents a night plus my only friend had marriage stars in her eyes. I didn't know anyone this side of the Atlantic and the ones I know on the other side have NO WAY of helping me! Arlene's on her way to Holland to choose the diamond Dean sent the money for and then to America. I don't even have anyone to talk to.

Please give me an answer to this.

I walked all the way from Gruenberg Park back to the youth hostel. I stopped on the bridge over the river to have a little talk with God. I have NEVER been in such a predicament in my LIFE! Desperation filled my heart as never before! I even had black thoughts of flinging myself off the bridge into the rushing river below! How selfish! That would only cause pain for the undeserving who would have to pull me out and tell my folks! What about my folks!? Well, I squelched that thought pronto!

Please, God, you've been there for me so many times. Please give me an answer to this. And I need it NOW! I even brought St. Jude, the Patron Saint of the Impossible, into the equation. There's just gotta be a way! Please St. Jude ...

At that moment, a military bus rumbled over the bridge. I hailed it down and asked the driver where he was headed and explained my plight. He recommended bus stops where all American busses stopped to pick up and drop off passengers to all the American installations in the area. Then he said, "Just tell the driver that you've left your pass at home or office ... maybe he'll take pity and give you a lift to the US Military personnel offices in the area." IT WORKED! Thank you, God, and St. Jude!

Do you take shorthand?

I started off the next day with hope in my heart and good intentions, and a list of all American installations I obtained at the first personnel office I'd visited. I covered a good half of all within reach of the busses. The drivers were all very compassionate and helpful. I'd do the other half of the offices the next day and surely there is ONE which had a position for an accountant or bookkeeper.

The first question I was asked at the personnel offices was, "Do you take shorthand?" I avoided it like a plague in high school. I knew I wanted to be ANYTHING BUT a secretary. Alas, I was sitting in the very last personnel office in the area at Rhine Main Airport, when an Air Force major walked in; looked at me and asked, "What are you doing here?"

I wanted to say, "What's it to ya, bro!" but didn't dare. I did proclaim to be looking for a job and this seemed to be the last stop possibility. He invited himself to sit down next to me and said, "My boss is looking for a secretary. Would you like me to introduce you?" With a tear in my eye and another in my heart I answered, "It would do no good. Everyone requires shorthand, the one skill I do not possess. I've been a bookkeeper for the government for years, but no one seems to need those skills here."

Yes, I'm desperate, but do I look like a fool?

"Well, young lady, since I perceive you must be at the end of your rope, may I recommend that you make an appointment with him anyway and who knows what he might come up with. I'd be happy to give you a ride to HQ USAFE."

"Thank you very much, Major. I'm familiar with the HQ USAFE." I wasn't, but I was desperate for ANYTHING. Little did I know at the time that HQ USAFE stood for Headquarters US Air Forces in Europe. "I'll be there at whatever time you can make the appointment." Yes, I was desperate, but did I look like a fool? For sure, I didn't fall off that turnip truck yesterday!

He set a time. I was there. So was he and the two single lieutenant colonels who worked in Colonel

Green's office. It was Friday before Labor Day. It seemed that the colonel was off on "White Ball Alert" with another colonel and two generals. Air Force officers are required to put in so much flight time to keep prepared for emergencies that may occur. I quickly learned what "White Ball Alert" was ... the four were off to golf in Spain!

We learned the colonel would be back in office Tuesday morning and an appointment was set. With a vestige of hope in my heart, I thanked them; said I'd see them Tuesday and gathered my belongings to return to my 50-cents-a-day hostel.

Colonel Green's secretary, Eleanor, asked me what I was doing for the Labor Day holiday. I explained that my traveling buddy was on her way home to get married and I was alone in the youth hostel with a bunch of Pakistanis and Egyptians.

Eleanor must have felt my loneliness in this moment and stopped me with, "Oh, please come back to Wiesbaden and spend the weekend with me." Music to my ears!

I went over to Frankfurt and made arrangements to return the following Tuesday afternoon. Laundered my best; packed and returned to meet her Saturday at the Amelia Earhart Hotel for Women, living facilities for those working at HQ US Air Forces in Europe. I eventually lived after I was employed.

The weekend made up in spades for being alone. Eleanor had a rollaway brought into her unit for me. She invited me to the Civilian Club, an old mansion atop a hill that made a most charming supper club. We registered for dinner and went into the bar for a cocktail. We found a seat at the bar when a handsome Texas drawl invited us to have a cocktail on him. That's when they announced that

Eleanor's table was ready. I thanked the Texan and said perhaps another time. He said, "Come back for an after-dinner drink. I'll be waiting."

Eleanor knew everyone in the club, and they all came by to see who I was. Hours passed. We ate; we drank; and we talked to everyone in the place. "Well, Eleanor, we'll never see that Texan again!" I said as we left the dining room.

Oh, but we did! Not only was he still waiting all those hours for us, he invited us both to the "Watch on the Rhine" the next day. A fun Sunday wine probe around the castles on the Rhine, with a lift to carry us to the peak. We all had a most delightful day and many more to follow. That's a story for another day in another chapter.

Well, young lady, I like your spunk!

Tuesday arrived ... and my interview with the colonel! We visited about the "White Ball Alert," where my travels had taken me all summer and we finally got around to that proverbial question that was raising havoc with my life, "Do you have shorthand?" I'd had it with that damn question and answered, "No, sir, but I can write really fast."

He took a draw on his big black cigar, let the smoke drift out and said, "Well, young lady, I like your spunk! If I were to change a secretary position to clerk typist until you could learn and pass the shorthand test required by civil service, then change it back to secretary when you'd passed the test, would you buy into it?"

"Absolutely! Oh yes! Would you? Could you REALLY do that for me?"

He did! I did! With my first paycheck, I bought a reel to reel recorder and practiced until I could truthfully say, "Yes, I can do shorthand ... the J C way." I worked for the War Plans colonel for three and one-half years at Headquarters United States Air Forces in Europe. Side note: I NEVER used shorthand except when I took other classes to learn other things not connected with USAFE. It was helpful to state I'd passed that civil service test. Though never using that skill, it paved my way to future employments. What a farce!

Back to the Civilian Club. It's rapid seating of Eleanor and me was a once in a lifetime experience. When I later became a member of the club; and was elected Treasurer of the Board, I NEVER got seated that quickly! Guess it was just one of those things meant to be!

The club had a great band which played on weekends and special occasions. When I'd walk into the club, the band always struck up "Hello, Dolly." I can never hear that song without a tear coming into my eye. When we returned to Germany years later, I drove up to the now empty manse, no longer a civilian club. HQ USAFE had moved to Ramstein Air Force Base. You know, I heard "Hello, Dolly!" softly pouring from that sad skeleton of yesteryear's joys and sat there and cried, looking out over the city and my heart spilling over with memoirs of yore!

Food for Thought ...

God grant me the serenity to accept the things that I cannot change; the courage to change the things I can change; and the wisdom to know the difference.

13

Drink From the Cup of Life Deeply and N'er Spill a Drop

1966-1970

It was a hard decision. I loved my freedom and the ability to do what I wanted when I wanted.

IN GERMANY, I had been given a mini-apartment housing in the Amelia Earhart nine story quarters for women only. Today it is a coed building. I was dating Gail Childers, a Texan and a microwave communications expert. His guidance was sought all over the world.

I met him my first weekend in Wiesbaden at the Civilian Club. Gail was headquartered in Wiesbaden and lived in an adorable little apartment in the heart of the shopping district. It had all the essentials. Walking was a delight—his apartment was within the famous Giant cuckoo clock.

He was transferred to Bangkok, Thailand, with Philco Ford. I remained in Germany. Soon after his departure, I received a ticket and a marriage proposal. It was a hard decision. I loved my freedom and the ability to do what I wanted when I wanted. But I loved the guy ... and, it was another part of the world I hadn't seen. We were married in Bangkok by a Thai amphur (the local legal) and registered with the American embassy.

I thought it was "doped" ... then it moved!

There were no civil service jobs in Bangkok, so I redirected my search and landed a position with a joint venture group: Dillingham based in Hawaii, Zachary in Texas and Kaiser in California and became the assistant personnel manager for transporting the American employees. In addition, I oversaw scheduling the company plane.

Rented from the Prime Minister
to Hong Kong—my Thai home.

My garden: in the back corner is a Spirit House, filled with
toy miniature animals that the "spirits" could ride on!

Many times, I was the maid of honor for employees
and acquired the skills and contacts to put together
weddings for the Americans who married in
Bangkok. Finally, it became my turn. Gail had to
make the proposal good. As many brides wonder—
am I doing the right thing? Count me in. That
same thought was running through my mind.
Did I really want to go through this again after

Johnny ditched me? It was my Irish friend who convinced me to go through with it. After all, my car and most of my stuff had been sold in Germany or sent to Kansas for storage and what I had was in Bangkok. I decided to stay. The Chaophya Hotel that housed the US military officers, aka the country club, was the site for our wedding.

International romance started in Germany.
Ate cake in Thailand!

I landed the cream job of the ages.

One day, my girlfriend, who also worked for Dillingham, Zachry, Kaiser, and I were playing the course just before the Christmas Holidays. Whom should we meet but BOB HOPE! He commented on our cute golf hats, calling them Easter bonnets and visited with us between shots. He and his entourage were headed to Vietnam to entertain the troops for which he was forever famous. He stayed at the Chaophya Hotel, the American Officers' Club, where Gail and I were married.

Elephant chairs for passengers! I brought a special one in Chiengmai and it's now in my home!

1970

Gail's job was finished in Thailand and we were off to Fort Washington, Pennsylvania, Philco Ford headquarters, where he trained for his next assignment: installing underwater cable to Taiwan. We found ourselves in America for a short eight months.

While Gail was learning how to navigate this new directive, I was left to walk the poodle couple and take care of the apartment. Anyone who knows me understands my need for something more vital. I noticed right across the street was Provident Indemnity Life Insurance Company. It just happened the president was seeking a new secretary. I interviewed and was hired, landing the cream job of the ages. It was so great, a friend quit her job to take mine when we left for Okinawa.

Beauregard and Wijitra add to our family
in Bangkok.

In Pennsylvania, our poodles surprised us with their
first litter of puppies the very night friends hosted
a farewell party for us. The "fur children" were so
nervous, we couldn't possibly leave them alone. We
took turns staying with them and attending the party.

Mom and pop poodles were my
traveling companions.

Gail went on to begin his job and find us a house. Since puppies need eight weeks with their mommy before entering a new home, I had a nice visit with Mom and Pop back in Kansas. All four of the dogs traveled from Pennsylvania to Kansas in crates on a plane. Since we were planning to stop off at my folks in Kansas on the way to Okinawa, it was a win-win. They fell in love with the little girl poodle, who naturally became theirs.

My cousin, a grad of the Veterinarian School at Kansas State, was in Manhattan from Florida attending a college reunion. He accompanied me to Kansas City to professionally send the baby boy off to friends back in Pennsylvania.

It was now my turn to head to Okinawa. Mom and pop poodles were my traveling companions.

We rented a house on a hill in Oyama, Okinawa, overlooking the East China Sea, with sunsets routinely coloring our skies. In fact, they weren't just sunsets, they were fantastic sunsets! When there were typhoons, we didn't let the storms get us down. We had typhoon parties. On our way, Gail had me sit on floor of the car. Anything that could be lifted by the wind was flying through the air and he didn't want me to get hit from the debris.

Gail was busy installing underwater cable from Okinawa to Taiwan and I accompanied him on several trips. Taiwan was famous for "pirated" records, tapes, oil paintings, art and books—copies that were produced very inexpensively and sold for pennies on the dollar—they were such bargains!

There were no jobs available for me on Okinawa, though there were Air force and Marine Military installations on the island which was at one time a hot spot in WWII. For the first time in my life, I was free to do anything I wished. For the very first time, I was a DEPENDENT! Someone was taking care of ME!

We had learned to golf in Germany and enjoyed playing in Thailand at the Royal Bangkok Sports Club. The club course was wrapped in and around the horse racetrack. They would run up a red flag for us to stop while the racing horses had the right of way. After they passed, a green flag signaled we could resume play. Certainly NOT like any other course we'd ever played. Unique and elegant.

In Okinawa, I was elected president of the Women's Golf Club twice; joined the other wives' club; decorated for holidays, etc., etc. I can tell it now, but at the time, it was a big dark secret. Many times, in the middle of a game, a spooky looking dark jet would zoom over; drop a packet of pictures taken of questionable areas; and zip back off at mock speed to spook some more. It was a covert operation to advise our troops of war-potential activities in area. We were all sworn to secrecy.

My plate was full ...

As prez, I arranged for a foursome of pro lady golfers to visit us between tournaments and demonstrate the finer skills they had perfected. We witnessed Penny Zavikas make a hole-in-one and were honored to help celebrate it at the "19th hole."

Another day, we played in the Okinawa International Tournament, with players from Taiwan and mainland China. One Taiwanese gentleman made a hole-in-one and invited us to come to play their course in Taiwan. We went and received red carpet treatment from the winner. Loved this type of international relations!

My plate was full ... I played golf every day for nearly two years but then guilt grabbed me, and I knew I had to do something of greater value. On Okinawa was Camp Kue Hospital, where our wounded troops were brought while waiting transport back home from Vietnam. It was calling to me.

I volunteered with Red Cross for anything I might do for them. I wrote their Christmas cards and letters back home; taught them macramé and other crafts. In general, I tried to give them a taste of home; reprieve from the battles they'd fought and friends they'd lost; and instill appreciation they so needed.

Some were wounded badly and looked to the volunteers' reactions as what they might anticipate from their wife, sis or mom. That was the toughest part! On my first day, I had to excuse myself; go outside and have a "Come to Jesus" talk with myself 'til I could handle this. Many suffered some serious injuries and needed our silent input and support!

For me, as I write this, my jaws tightened.

The "event" ended. Everyone was going home one way or another! Gail was still busy installing cable to Taiwan. Camp Kue Hospital asked if I'd work with the dope addicts. OR if I'd give them five full days a week FREE, they'd teach me enough physical therapy to help injured rehabilitate. I chose the latter and absolutely LOVED it.

If I could have a "do-over," I'd be a physical therapist! How very rewarding to see one recoup the broken body and make a life again. We treated horrific burn cases, and horrendous war injuries and their lives became whole and worth living. So many give up hope when there's an answer just waiting. They all needed positive mental attitudes to make it through these toughest parts of their lives. What we could give them in that direction was worth every minute spent.

For me, as I write this, my jaws tightened. During WWII, there were hidden bunkers along the shoreline, each loaded with weapons aimed at our troops, many of which the Japanese took out. But what got me was that after the war, the US gave Okinawa back to the Japanese. We were on a golf course as streams of cars went by on flatbeds that had been set aflame by disgruntled Okinawans who were seeking revenge when their country, and they, were taken over by the Japanese. The time was Christmas and to this day, I still wonder if those cars had presents in them for little ones.

Gail's underwater cable to Taiwan finished. Germany ... here we come!

1970-1972

While living in the German Mountain Village of Taunusstein Hahn, one of the young men working for my husband received a surprise Christmas package from his aunt in Virginia—a Smithfield ham. He was perplexed about what he was going to do with this big hunk of meat. After all he was a bachelor and there are just so many ham sandwiches a guy can handle.

"Fear not, Jeffrey," said I. "If you're willing to share your fortune, I shall make the Southern special meal of black-eyed peas and ham for New Year's Day and all the folks with the company, neighbors and friends can enjoy." And off I sat to find a recipe for the supposedly good luck meal.

Jumped into my little red bug and headed out to find a recipe. HQ USAFE had just moved to Ramstein but hadn't moved the library yet. They had a cookbook with the recipe I needed ... or so

I thought! It stated that one should buy frozen black-eyed peas and there was a recipe on the package. I had just purchased a pretty good supply of dried black-eyed peas. Of course, there was NO recipe on the package! Mom had always made beans from the dried. Only thing I could do in the limited time I'd been given was call Mom in Junction City!

After a nice visit on the phone and advice from the "Master Chef," I felt I was ready to soak the peas overnight and get 'er going. However, I was not aware of how the Smithfield's preserved their hams using mega salt!

We had a goodly supply of German wines and beers. After all, we were in Germany! Platters of slaw—cabbage is part of the meal—and cornbread that helped to "tame" the over-salted meat down a bit. No one complained and everyone had fun.

Many carried the traditional meal on for years after. We certainly did!

Seems I always learn things the hard way. Black-eyed peas became a tradition in our home every New Year's. A big pot of black-eyed peas and all the other condiments, along with plenty of German wine and beer are great while watching football! The peas and "unsalted" ham get better each year. Black-eyed peas, anyone?

1972

Returning to Germany from Okinawa required finding affordable housing for the Childers and their white French Poodle, Beauregard. We mourned the loss of Wijitra, our mamma poodle who died of leptospirosis while in Okinawa. It was the only time I ever saw Gail cry. An "unfurnished" unit—be it an apartment, condo, townhouse or house in America was far different than what Germany offered. The unfurnished interpretation meant bare walls and minimum plumbing. Forget light features, faucets or the items you would think were essential and must have's. I'm talking quasi-camping.

Finding a place to live this time was a far cry from the first. We knew we'd be there less than a year. We needed a furnished place that would meet our needs 'til our household goods caught up with us, months later.

While having lunch with old friends still there, I learned of a potential furnished rental. It seems a couple had decided to "split the sheet" and hadn't decided who got what. If they could find the right tenant, it could work for all. Fortunately, we were the "right" tenant—even with Mr. Beauregard. Poodles were beloved and have a priority in Germany. They're invited into restaurants and treated like honored guests often served before their "human parents."

The furnished end townhouse was in Taunusstein Hahn, a charming mountain village in the forest area north of Wiesbaden. It was delightfully furnished even to the cuckoo clock on the wall; clouds of comfy feather-filled duvets on the beds and schranks to replace missing closets. It seems insurance on a closet is as great as that for an entire room, as it is considered a room. Schranks were heavy and huge wooden pieces of furniture which fulfill the closet needs.

A bonus for us happened—the house even had a garage. When our furniture and belongings arrived from Okinawa, it saved us costly storage fees. What a win-win!

Christmas was coming with lots of guests from hither, thither and yonn anticipated. Alas, all the holiday décor was not to arrive 'til the coming year sometime. Gotta do something about that!

117

I stood in the front yard discussing it with Mr. Beauregard when a lightbulb went off! The front storm door to our townhome was a large sheet of heavy glass. Germans don't have doorknobs like those in America.

My gift—they became lifelong friends.

L. Gene captured me when I managed a leather goods shop in the American Officers Hotel in Wiesbaden, Germany.

The pusher on the storm door was a piece of
polished wood. I took off the red mitten I was
wearing and slipped it over the pusher. In my
mind's eye was a jolly fat Santa Clause reaching
out his hand in holiday greetings. Beauregard and
I jumped into my VW and buzzed into the village
to pick up art supplies to bring Santa alive. He was
adorable and introduced us to many new neighbors
we had the fortune to meet.

The darling little Habermann family with 6-year-
old son Patrick and 7-year old daughter Yvonn were
headed to the forest across the street to walk their
dog, Schluftel. Curiosity brought a tap on the door
with, "Where did you get that fat St. Nicholas?"
Heading to their home with my art supplies, a jolly
Santa was created on their door. My gift—they
became lifelong friends.

Mom Habermann, Sylvia, and her sister came to
visit me in Kansas. And when Yvonn finished high

school in Germany, Sylvia called to ask if I would host Yvonn for three months to allow her to pick up American English.

"Of course, send her on over." Sylvia brought her and I set about getting her enrolled in a language class. Junction City is a military town and many of the foreign military brides are offered language courses. This really didn't fit this pretty petite German lass.

Instead, I reached out to my cousin. She was on the school board and suggested other choices. We got Yvonn enrolled in Junction City High School. She earned an American diploma from my alma mater and made lifelong friends with Dr. Kaldor's red-headed twins plus one and their pink convertible. She went to her one and only prom with a good lookin' "tall drink of water." I gave her my class ring some years later when she came for

Christmas. The very best thing of all, my mother
became an Oma ... German for grandmother.
A prideful title she'd naught have had if not for
Santa in Taunusstein Hahn.

Today, Yvonn represents Lufthansa as a flight
attendant. She bought an apartment in Hochheim,
Germany, and was able to fly down to Florence,
Italy, to take my best friends and me to lunch when
we did a Mediterranean cruise in 2019. She loves
seeing the world and routinely shares pics of all her
travels with me. We are in constant communication
via text, email and WhatsApp that is free to use.
That little 7 year old is in her 50s now!

God replaced the babies I couldn't have and did
a splendid job of picking only the best. I have a
special room in my heart for each of them: Yvonn,
Jennifer, Hannah Rose, Madi, Nancy, Joy, Adam,
Ethan and Scott. Each is a gift. And I was not

responsible for diapering or sending any to college— just sharing love and respect for each! Love 'em ALL.

Food for Thought ...

You cannot use up creativity! The more you use it—the more you have!

14

Germany to the USA

1973

*Clicking my heels as I left my meeting, I just knew
that I could do this.*

THE "EVENT" ENDED in Vietnam and the
employment scene changed drastically. No more
jobs such as we had enjoyed abroad for eleven years.
Gail and I return to America, choosing to relocate
in Junction City, Kansas, where I was born during
those Depression years. My parents were delighted
to have their only chick and her rooster home for
good. When we arrived, there was a freeze on civil
service jobs at Fort Riley. The hope for adding time
toward retirement thwarted.

With Gail's managerial skills, he was fortunate to obtain the building manager job at Fort Riley, where he oversaw the building of a 1,001 housing unit programmed for the expansion of the fort. It was a blessing which kept us afloat until we moved from my folks' tiny—but free—basement apartment into my great grandparents' house—one that we rented from their estate. Finally, we made it into a home of our own.

Meanwhile, I sold Avon products to provide Christmas gifts for that first Christmas at home after missing so many while abroad. Avon was so impressed with my selling skills that they offered me a managerial position. Off to Kansas City I flew for an interview and attempted to grasp an immediate answer from them. The result was: I had a big decision to make.

The management team had an offer that was so good, it was hard to pass up ... but I did! I had just passed the state real estate licensure after self-teaching myself using the book by David Semenow. Yes, it had been a struggle, but I HAD DONE IT!

Clicking my heels as I left my meeting, I just knew that I could do this.

Thanking Avon for the offer, I promised the team if after a year I'd made the wrong choice in real estate, I would accept their generous offer. They compassionately accepted my answer and wished me the best and said that they'd wait the year.

Clicking my heels as I left my meeting, I just knew that I could do this and joined Barnhill/Brown Real Estate and never looked back. When one has a serious decision to make about anything, I've found it's best to take a big sheet of paper and write down on one side all the positive aspects of the decision to be made and down the other all the negatives.

Weigh each well. Consult an expert if appropriate on any you have a question or concern about. Think about it ... sleep on it ... pray about it. And make the best decision God and your gut guides you to. Then, live with it. I did ... and I've never been sorry. Ironically, it was my Avon customers who led me to my first three real estate listings and sales.

Real estate was my thing. And, within a few years, I was ready to fly the nest and sprout my own business ownership wings and train my agents as Earl Brown trained me. I taught them all I knew and encouraged them to be the best they could be. Two of them opened their own offices as I had! At least my competition had all the tools they needed to be the best they could be. I was very proud of them as Earl had been of me.

Food for Thought ...

Lead with passion! Happiness never decreases by being shared. Many candles can be lit from one.

15

J C Realty, Inc.

1978

It turned out that Gail was definitely "not good enough" with his cards!

AFTER FIVE YEARS training with Earl Brown, the best real estate broker in the world, I decided I was ready to "Do it My Way." Gail and I bought a house at 720 W. 5th, in Junction City, aka known by the locals as "J C." The entire block was zoned commercial so I could do an in-home office arrangement until I could afford a "Window on Mainstreet." Though lacking certain qualities that make it a home, primarily privacy, it did have location—smack in the heart of J C—which continues still. For me, it became the heart of both "JC"—Junction City—and yours truly.

When the world becomes a jungle out there, isn't it great to have a Realtor who can contain the beast?

Gail built us a large family room off the back of the house, and we used the finished basement for our "home only." It was great for a few years, but difficult wearing "two hats" with the same chimney.

1980

When the Edge of England Fish and Chip Restaurant became available on the main thoroughfare in town, I talked to the owner, Fred Bramlage, about purchasing it. Fred is a family friend; one of the most highly respected businessmen in JC; a good friend of mine. A deal was done!

In that shake-roofed, diamond-windowed perfect location had been a fish market for years. There was an essential need to erase all remnants of its previous use. That fish fragrance had to be totally mitigated. My cousin in construction managed the transition magnificently. He poured new concrete throughout; added extra sheet rock and ceiling tiles; and then added new carpeting.

Décor and special homey touches were next on my list. As I was driving down one of the neighborhoods, I spied a little dollhouse sitting on the front lawn.

I knocked on the owners' door to inquire if they might be interested in selling it. The woman said she'd give it to me if I'd sell her house.

The local kids loved it and encouraged their parents to go to "J C's" little house when looking for a new home.

Movin and Groovin ... I found this treasure in a woman's yard. She gave it to me when I sold her house.

Wow! A double win! Hauled the "Little Minnie Me" away to be renovated; sold her house for a happy profit; and found the perfect replacement for her changed needs. We were all VERY happy!

Then, I hired a pro to install a tall, strong pole to include a changeable reader board that announced properties for sale. Pop was a sign painter, now gone to God. The signage he created included a long magnetic pole. I added a large letter/number inventory that was purchased. I personally changed those numbers and letters frequently with houses for sale and holiday greetings.

The little "Minnie Me" by now was ready to be installed atop the pole on a turning platform. It was definitely cute with its fresh coat of white, red shutters, blue roof and lights within like a Thomas Kinkade painting. The local kids loved it and encouraged their parents to go to "J C's" little house when looking for a new home. The little ones also loved the playroom inside with boxes of toys, Shirley Temple movies and finished jig saw puzzles on the walls. My secretary was a huge asset. She adored kids and looked after the young'uns while their parents went shopping for a new home.

Gail's housing project had ended. Next on his list was the local Tastee Freeze—his favorite haunt for burgers and shakes. After owning it for a few years and decided that his teenage staff could do all the management. Gail said, "I've got better burgers to flip!" The country club would be his "next project"— as in hanging out with the boys and playing cards. While he was dealing the cards, the teen staff gave away the farm—burger by burger; shake by shake to all their pals.

It turned out that Gail was definitely "not good enough" at cards! One evening, he announced that he was heading to Texas for a job interview. Days later, I received a call—not from Texas ... this one was from Las Vegas. He was broke and needed money. "Broke … what do you mean you are broke … and in Vegas?"

"I'll tell you all about it when I get home." Foolishly, I sent him a few hundred dollars by Western Union.

That was quickly followed with a phone call the next day. "I'm broke."

"I don't understand what you are doing … and what you are doing in Vegas."

Both angry and perplexed, I knew what my next step would be. I sent Gail something, but not what he expected. It was a one-way airplane ticket to return home.

Before the plane landed, I had more phone calls and mail. Not from Gail. From bankers right here in Junction City! They wanted money too! To my dismay, they revealed that he had used both my property and my company as collateral for thousands of dollars I knew nothing about. Nor did I sign for— he had forged my signatures on documents and checks.

I needed to say "Adios" to both the bankers and Gail. The plot thickened. One of those teens from the Tastee Freeze was now working at the bank and was delighted to cash any checks that Gail produced. Signatures were irrelevant.

Turning to my attorney, he did his magic. Not only did I get an "emergency divorce" within 24 hours … he nailed the bankers as well. I was reimbursed for all the forged checks and my properties were released.

With Gail gone, and my good name restored, I was elected to the Junction City's City Commission and became a very active member of the J C Chamber of Commerce. Being a "solo" was good for me and I was now on a roll, popping up everywhere.

My renovated office building and signage won a prize from the Chamber of Commerce. Along with all the combined activities that I was engaged in at Fort Riley and JC, I also served on the USO Board; joined the Officers Wives Club; and was even named "Honorary MP" by MP General Chidickamo, with whom I assisted in presenting honors once a month to the troops.

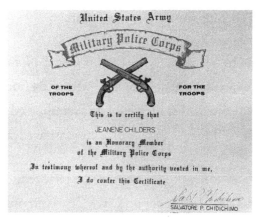

I was thrilled! Of course, I accepted!

One of the most active groups at the Chamber was the "Old Trooper Group." Fort Riley was the Old Army Cavalry Post. A statue of "Old Trooper" (the last horse) graced the parade field to remind all of the original purpose of the Cavalry Post. It was totally testosterone—only men members. Fred Bramlage, Town "Father" and President of "Old Trooper," invited me to be the first woman member.

I was thrilled! Of course, I accepted! The main purpose was to play host to higher ranking incoming officers to Fort Riley. There was a nice luncheon at the Country Club to express our appreciation for their new assignment and offer the services and key of our "Sister City."

My first experience with the Country Club lunch was with the arrival of a new colonel. I was at the bar ordering a libation when a retired full colonel, working at the local bank and married to the banker's widow, put himself directly into my face

saying, "Well! Women are just everywhere!"
Then he proceeded to explain that the "Old
Trooper" was just businessmen. "What are you
doing here, Little Lady?" He was terribly rude!
Hearing the colonel's indignation and rant, a
retired 3-star general, who along with his 2-star
brother and their wives had retired in Junction
City, put the colonel in his place properly.

"Dan, as I understand, your bank sponsors you to
be here. Jeanene is here by personal invitation of
Fred Bramlage, who has invited her to be the first
woman member. I recommend you apologize and
consider that she and her J C Realty, Inc., paid and
sponsored her membership. Also remember her
contributions to the many organizations at
Fort Riley, as well as J C. Did you know that her
grandfather and Fred's father worked together as
blacksmiths, shoeing Old Trooper and the 7th
Cavalry? She belongs if anyone does!"

Then, a few months later, Fort Riley and the Chamber's Old Trooper Group welcomed the FIRST woman general to Fort Riley. Don't know if it was his choice—it certainly was NOT MINE—the Nasty colonel was seated next to me at the luncheon. Oh, how I wanted to say, "Yes, Dan, women ARE everywhere!" I pride myself with only delivering that message silently to myself. I just smiled sweetly at Dan and the new 3rd region ROTC general.

Some while later, I became friends with the general. I shared the story with her, never revealing who he was. She revealed that this happened to her lots of times. Familiar with the climb in military rank, I was amazed that she had been made one of the highest ranking women in the military at that time. She had no partner preparing great parties to push her ahead. She did it all herself and was well-deserving. No wonder she was a general!

General Myrna Williamson and I became, and still are, very best friends. We shared trips to DC for special events and meetings. After I had been elected a Junction City commissioner, I represented the city in many military and civic meetings.

My mother, along with her brother and their little poodles were killed in a truck/car wreck in February of 1987. Myrna had been making a speech to a ROTC Group. She was just landing when her pilot informed her about Mother. She was at my door STAT! Offering anything she could do and truly meaning it.

Food for Thought ...

Difficult roads often lead to beautiful destinations.

16

Washington, DC ...
Here I Come to the Army
Material Command HQ

1987-1991

*There were five generals honoring me with their
presence at my special retirement party.*

FINALLY, I ARRIVE in Washington, DC, to
claim it as a residence after years of "visiting" it for
conferences connected with the military.

The first place I interviewed for a job was the Army
Material Command in Alexandria, Virginia. It
was ideal and within view from my bedroom.
A completely unusual location considering where
other potential jobs could have landed.

What did I ever do to deserve that!

I liked what I saw and what I heard and immediately accepted the job, starting within days. I was assigned Mrs. M.D.! Now who was Mrs. M.D.? Picture this: a flaming redhead with a temper and manner to match. A combination of a diva and tyrant to boot. What did I ever do to deserve that!

Those of us who interacted with her referred to her as a GS-fantastic—all the government positions started with the code "GS"... the fantastic is what she proclaimed she was. She was the Chief of Interns. Ideally, this is a position, meaning you are at the bottom and the only place you could go was up. Right? Nope, not if you were me. When I work with or for others, my goal was always to get along, to smooth things when it gets bumpy. For Mrs. M.D., she was damned if she let me move anywhere.

She wanted me to be hers ... and only hers! Routinely, she'd appear at the last minute after charging up Highway 1 and toss her keys on my desk. The next thing out of her mouth was a demand that I go move her car. And sigh, I did.

Mrs. M.D. was a real pain in the kazoo! Mine and everyone else's. When I wasn't around, she'd park in handicap areas and challenge anyone, threatened them if they attempted to move her car—everyone knew her car—it was her modus operandi!

One day, Big Al showed up. All the women who worked for her were gathered around her already hoisted vehicle to a tow truck, thrilled with the prospect that she would get her due. They were sweet talking Big Al to take her car off and look the other way. He went into bargaining mode and told them that he would do it ... but there was a condition as he put out his hand. The girls ended up digging into their purses, gathering a collection amongst

themselves and transferring it to Big Al's outstretch
hand. After the tow truck had left the parking lot,
one of the girls placed the car keys on her desk.

Occasionally, she'd have me go with her to the
airport to bring her car back to long-term parking
for her return, then someone would pick me up.
She drove to Reagan Airport whilst putting on
makeup and mascara. One poke in the eye and we'd
go flying off the pike. Really kinda scary in beltway
traffic. Not surprisingly, her steering wheel was
painted in various shades of nail polish she'd apply
doing a manicure to and from home.

Finally, I could take it no more. One of the gals
with connections helped me get a job in the
Pentagon in the office of the Secretary of Defense
from which I retired three years later. And what a
beautiful retirement party they threw me at a
penthouse restaurant. Everyone I knew in the area
came plus a few I'd known from other parts of the

world—even my ski buddies from Germany including a three-star general. I was delighted to include friends from the Pentagon Toastmasters Club, which was the first ever to invite women to become Toastmasters. Actually, it should have been called ToastMASTERS ... since it was originally was all men. Prior to that time, there were Toastmistresses and Toastmasters and never the twain had met.

"You Have Touched So Many Hearts."

Some great stories came out of that group, which included old, retired top-ranking officers from every branch. There were five generals honoring me with their presence at my special retirement party. And my boss in the Pentagon, Tommy Tucker, had asked what I'd like for a retirement gift. I replied: a rose bush. It was there in full bloom as purchased by Mrs. Tucker, his wife. Melba Lyons, Junction

145

City High School classmate living in Bel Air,
Maryland, and the man in her life were there as
well. We slipped away after lunch to tour the
Washington Cathedral.

Thanking those who came to the luncheon ... love it that
Stan is listening with rapt attention.

There were beautiful pieces of crystal and lotsa
flowers. I never knew so many cared so much about
me. My big surprise was the appearance of Mrs.
M.D. with a dozen long stem thorn-free roses and

a Precious Moment figurine, stating "You Have Touched So Many Hearts." Of course, the roses were red ... you could have pushed me over with a pin when I got that!

Sharing a toast with my boss, Tommy Tucker.

The penthouse restaurant was full and a whole lotta love going around! Ya never know how things can end up if you keep smiling! What a day. And Stan the Man was there, by my side.

Love it that Brig. General Myrna Williamson,
a Silver Fox, celebrated with me.

Food for Thought ...

I always try to believe the best in everybody ...
it saves so much trouble.

17

The Four Silver Foxes

1985 to present

*The glue that held us all together from
the beginning was Myrna.*

ONE OF MY favorite TV shows was, and still is,
The Golden Girls. Well, permit me to introduce you
to the "Four Silver Foxes." Ladies of achievement,
daring and thirsting for adventure, and with great
senses of humor, proving themselves every day in
every way. Our current ages are 83 to 92—one
widow, three divorcees—and we're still going
strong. Just imagine what we four were like three
decades ago! The glue that held us all together from
the beginning was Myrna.

We loved Sturgis, South Dakota!

Meet Myrna Hennrich Williamson

Most people called Myrna Ma'am or General ... she was always, and still is, Myrna to me. We met at a special Chamber of Commerce "Old Trooper" reception held in her honor at the Junction City Country Club.

As a single female general, she would be invited to many social events and needed escorts. After all, a lady general just can't date "anyone," can she? Usually, a trusted friend is pulled in to "help" when a "someone" was needed. I was the trusted friend. On one "help" call, she asked me if I would introduce her to someone who could act as her escort for a special celebration. I introduced her to Dr. Alex Scott, a close friend. Truth be told, I had a bit of a thing for him ... but it was not to be. He became smitten with her.

As a city commissioner, I often found myself in Washington, DC. When there, Myrna and I shared a hotel suite where she in turn, invited all her cronies to join us.

Myrna is a retired Army brigadier general and recipient of South Dakota's most prestigious award. In 2012, she was inducted into the South Dakota Hall of Fame. Myrna was the highest ranking woman in the Army at the time of retiring in the 1990s and the only female general ever to be stationed at Fort Riley, Kansas. She oversaw the the eight state 3rd Region ROTC.

Myrna lives between her penthouse in Springfield, VA, and a beautiful lake house in Madison, South Dakota, and a pied á terre in Sioux Falls.

One of the things that I loved about her was her dedication to her nieces and nephews. Her brother was a Frito Lay driver with eight kids—not a Mormon or Catholic—just a sexy Protestant in a very cold winter state! Myrna made a promise: if any of his kids wanted a university education, she would make it happen. Six of the eight took her up on it. Then she added a bonus: if they graduated, they got a dream trip of their choice.

Meet Dona Hilderbrand

Dona is a retired Air Force colonel of 25 years. She served 20 years abroad—England, Thailand

and Germany. After her retirement, she and her Air Force colonel husband (now deceased) settled in Monument, Colorado, where she still lives.

When it was time to enhance the beautiful hardwood floors in their new home, Dona knew the perfect carpet and where to get it. Now, I'm not talking about going to the local store. I'm talking about a long plane ride—as in Hong Kong. While in Hong Kong, she met Myrna through mutual friends. The two of them shopped for oriental rugs for Dona's home in Colorado.

Dona was an avid hiker all her life and participated in the Bolder Boulder. Today, her physical running days are behind her ... but she manages to keep a trio of assistants running—taking care of her needs so she can remain in her home off the golf course in Monument. She still hikes in the forest that abuts her property ... with one of the assistants trailing behind her! Monthly, she attends events at the Air Force Academy and is delighted to be one of the presenters of awards to students there.

Dona is a collector of all things—from treasures to trash. One of her personal favorites is to discover what's behind the doors and under tables in second-hand shops. It's her mecca. One time, she needed to make room in her home to add "more finds." We took beautiful silver services, silverware for 24 one day to a very high-end consignment shop in Denver where they offered her a lot of money. Not ever having children, she chose to redirect it, giving all proceeds to the Children's Hospital.

Meet Judy Farris

A South Dakotan who has never lived out of the state of South Dakota, Judy was the perfect tour guide of all things South Dakota and can recite its history backward and forward. If anyone desires information about monuments and visitor activities, she's the perfect person to have on the phone ... or by your side.

Judy and Myrna were elementary school classmates, eventually graduating from high school together. Their paths took them to the military where Myrna went into leadership and Judy remained, working with ex-military women and their children in filling their housing and employment needs.

If you walked into her home, you would think you were at a network television station. You see, Judy is an avid sports fan who just happens to have four TVs lined up and on at the same time, so she won't miss a game, ever or anywhere.

Outside of her love of sports ... it's the Denver Stock Show that brings her into my neck of the woods every year. Her personal fave: the bucking broncos.

As I was putting the finishing touches on this book, I received a call from Myrna. Our dear friend Judy had beat us to the Rainbow Bridge saying her last goodbye on April 21, 2020.

Meet Jeanene "J C" Childers

That's me ... the chauffer of the "Four Silver Foxes." One year, it was a two week tour of South Dakota. Of course, it was conducted by Judy. Another year, it was a Colorado Springs gathering at Monument's Pikes Peak tour that was not successful. The weather turned nasty and we turned back. Another time Dona gave us a colonel's behind the scenes tour of the Air Force Academy and all of Colorado Springs. We also had a fabulous week in Grand Lake, Colorado, at the home of Arlene Zick, one of my long-time friends and owner of Lake Haven Lodge.

We had some fun when we encountered the "big guy"!

The glue that held the Four Silver Foxes together from the beginning was Myrna.

Food for Thought ...

To have a friend, you first must be one. Set an example to the world that you are a friend by being your own BFF. After all, you really are—maybe more. Who really cares about the outcome of your life other than you?

Care deeply for those in need. Feed the hungry. Give solace to the worried. Do something everyday for someone else, and, hopefully, unbeknownst to them.

The sneaky secret helps the angels who set the path to love. Love yourself. Love your neighbor. Love the woeful. Love the cheery. They are all God's children. What you do for them, you do for Him.

18

Meet STAN ... THE MAN ... Whatta Ride!

1988

Well, Hello there!

I REALLY WONDERED about the new people in my life in DC. After boarding the elevator each morning at Army Material Command Headquarters, I'd smile; look around at each of the other passengers and say in my sweetest Kansas way, "Good Morning!" It never failed. Absolute silence prevailed and I felt as if each was accusing me of killing his grandma!

What's with these people? Are they all in fear of losing their jobs and they think I'm aiming to

make that happen? Not to be deterred, I continued my friendly greeting each day. I was certain SOMEONE in that elevator would answer me! Don't know how long I continued this before a friendly masculine voice came out of the corner of the elevator with "Well, hello there!" That made my morning.

New Year's Eve 2016 ... What a night!

Who was this voice? I wondered. Getting off on
the same floor, he introduced himself to me.
The month of March was embedded in my mind
forward. He was Stan and his office was right
across the hall from mine. He was a graphic artist.
One day, he came into my office to borrow a
dictionary. As he stood there looking at it,
upside down mind you, I offered him my readers.
"Oh, I don't need glasses!"

"Then, pray tell, why is the book you are looking
at upside down?"

He accepted the glasses; turned the book right side
up; looked up a word; then invited me out Friday
for dinner and a movie. It was drizzling rain as we
walked along the Potomac under an umbrella in
Old Town Alexandria. The movie, *Gorillas in the
Mist* was the rather appropriate movie we saw
that evening.

Stan was a handsome Sean Connery look-alike.

Movies became a Friday night date, interspersed with occasional trips to the Virginia beaches along with art shows and museums and theater performances. Stan lived in his house in Arlington, three miles from the Pentagon and I shared the three-story townhome with Brigadier General Myrna Williamson in Alexandria. We were all busy with our jobs and social lives.

And so it went for the seven years I lived in Virginia. We had a solid friendship and wanted nothing more.

Arlene, my old roommate and European traveling buddy of 1962 and hubby, Dean Zick, whom I frequently visited, encouraged me to return to

Colorado. Their three "kids" had left the nest and were off to colleges or marriage. They were rattling around their large home and had plenty of room for me to stay as long as I wished.

Arlene never cooked when we were the four roommates of years past. She was always being wined and dined and brought us doggy bags in lieu of cooking. Having three kids and a hungry hubby changed all that. Dean was delighted to have me join them. Arlene outdid herself proving her culinary skills and he ate it up! And so did I!

Stan missed me. He was on a plane that first Christmas and every three months after that until he retired and joined me permanently in Colorado. Meanwhile, I'd found a fixer-upper home in the Pinery area of Parker, Colorado, which Stan and I bought together. Now, it was my turn and I'd started renovating.

Stan was a handsome Sean Connery look-alike with a beautiful full head of white hair and a beard to match. I'd tried for years to encourage him to play Santa. When I learned he was coming for Christmas, I decided to make him a Santa outfit, which turned out to be red joggers and a Santa hat—a perfect outfit that would work for the Zick's eight grandkids.

When I picked him up at the Colorado Springs Airport, we learned the airline had lost his luggage. We were headed directly to the Zick's 12 bedroom lakeside lodge in Grand Lake for the holidays. No time to shop. The airlines had a shuttle service deliver his bag to Grand Lake in the mountains days later. Meanwhile, he strolled the village in what looked like Santa in red long johns. He was teased forever about that.

We loved takeout. Stan got out his pen and added me
to the dinner atmosphere.

Finally, his missing clothing arrived, and we had
a marvelous Holiday. Grand Lake was frozen.
We could walk across from the Boat House into
the village without fear of falling in.

Should I head for the snow-filled
ditch on the right?

Returning from Grand Lake on New Year's Day, we were turned back at the pass. The main ski slope in Winter Park was known as Mary Jane. It was experiencing avalanches. All of the traffic was redirected to the Eisenhower Tunnel and it was snowing hard with freezing conditions. We called from Granby to advise the group still in the lodge of our plight. The backseat was full with the luggage of friends from California and Zick's old dog, Rowdy.

Just past Granby, I had a quick choice to make. An approaching truck from the other side was sliding onto our side of the road. Get hit? Or, should I head for the snow-filled ditch on the right? Quickly, I veered toward the ditch! Airbags went off and the car appeared on fire and filling with smoke. Sitting at a slant in the ditch, I yelled for Stan to get out and come around to the driver's side to get Rowdy, who had slid to the floor, and me out. When Stan reached for him, Rowdy's "thanks" was to bite Stan in his beard, then jumping out onto the road with Stan in pursuit.

A sheriff, who just happened on the scene, pulled over. He helped Stan capture Rowdy and put dog and me in the backseat of his police car. Now if you've never been in the back seat of a police car, which I hadn't, I quickly learned that it locks occupants in automatically. Half the backseat was full of his paraphernalia and less than half a seat held a very large, very anxious dog—and ME!

Meanwhile, Stan and the sheriff called a tow truck to pull my year old Honda into the car repair lot. It was declared 100% destroyed—totaled—because of the twisted undercarriage. Then, he called the lodge to tell them what had happened and that we needed a ride down the mountain.

The next morning, I borrowed Dean Zick's car to get Stan back down to the Springs for his flight back to DC. Roads were still iffy, and I was quite anxious after totaling my car, but we made it! There were bets that Stan would never come back after I'd nearly killed him.

Threat of death did not deter him. He returned every three months until he retired from Civil Service and moved to Colorado permanently. We bought a fixer-upper house in the Pinery I still call "Home."

Stan the Man, became my main squeeze for the next 23 years!

Stan was known as "Parker's Napkin Artist." Though gifted with sketch pads of all sizes and descriptions, he favored restaurants' paper napkins to display his talents. We would go out to dinner where he would notice a child acting up and approach the table with a napkin; encourage the child to draw three lines on the napkin; then ask a child what his or her favorite animal was. In a flash, that animal would appear on the napkin to the astonishment of the child and parents alike.

Stan always gave his drawings to kids. This is of Blackie.

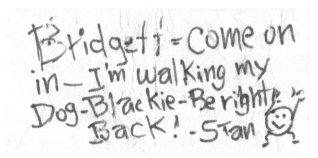

I loved his notes that he left for visitors on our front door!

Children weren't his only admirers. He loved to sketch lovely ladies and gift them with their portraits, always bringing out their best features. Many have told me they framed them and favored them over other pictures. Some of the children retained their animal pictures as well.

Stan was diagnosed with diabetes and "early onset" dementia. Into each life some rain must fall! I was his caregiver, researching how to make what time he had left the best it could be. We spent a lot of time at doctors and hospitals. It's part of life, but we made the best of it together. There are wonderful support groups and books.

All was well until September 10, 2017, when he went to join the angels. He rests today high on a hill mid-Parker, overlooking the snow-capped Rockies to the west and the Tailgate to the east— our favorite place to dance and dine.

One of our last photos together, 2017.

When I asked Stan where he wanted to go at the end, his answer: "with you!" And I replied, "Honey, I'm not ready just yet, but when the time comes, I'll be with you. The spot we chose is large enough to include my heart along with your boot and hat, plus kitchen linens inscribed 'Together Forever!' Even including a couple of hot pads! You never know!"

171

Inscribed on the brass plate at Stan's resting place is "Parker's Napkin Artist." Come sit on the bench and look at the mountains to the west and Main-street Parker's Tailgate to the east. We'll be dancing on a cloud with all our dogs we bade farewell along the way. Ironically, a picture of the very spot turned up from somewhere by surprise to lead you to our bench. Sit and rest awhile and think about "what you are going to do with the rest of your life. Drink from the cup of life deeply—and n'er spill a drop!

Life is not a journey to the grave, with the intention of arriving safely in a pretty and well-preserved body. But rather, sliding in broadside, thoroughly worn out and proclaiming loudly: "WOW, WHATTA RIDE!"

Food for Thought ...

How very fortunate I am. God has given me so much, and I can share it freely with others. Each gift magnifies the gifts inside yourself.

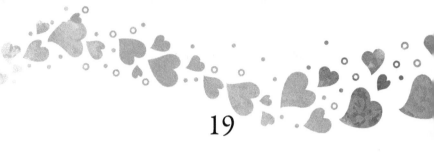

19

BLACKIE and STAN

2015

*I'm here. I'm making Stan get off the sofa
and walk me.*

MY "BONUS" DAUGHTER, Nancy has a heart
as big as the whole wide world. She is especially
fond of dogs for whom space is limited and who
are facing euthanasia if a place for them cannot be
found. Though a busy Realtor, mom, and wife, she
MAKES time in her life to help these poor critters.
Her mission is to find homes and folks who will
temporarily care for them 'til they can be placed in
forever homes.

Both Nancy and I are a pair who cannot watch
those heart-rendering eyes on TV and in shelters

begging to be rescued. Their sad, tearful eyes cut right into our hearts—and I bet yours as well. One time Nancy was seeking a temp home for a Border Collie being flown down from Utah and asked if we'd keep him until someone would give him a "Forever Home." That January, we'd lost our 17-year-old Sheltie, Duncan. His mate, Gracie, was lonely, and we thought: why not? The two could keep each other company.

It takes rain to make rainbows.

When Nancy opened the back of her van and then a cage, releasing a HUGE one hundred eleven pound black and white animal! Border Collies are half or less than that size! Wow, he's a BIG feller! Certainly larger than we anticipated! He looked like a Great Pyrenees! Even the vet thought that when we took him for his first appointment.

It was late and Nancy had nowhere to turn to seek help. She already had several dogs in her house. Stan and I agreed to keep him temporarily, certain that we'd find a farm that would welcome the big guy. The bonus was that he and Gracie got along fine.

Stan and his best buddy, Blackie.

We searched and searched, but no place was turning up to welcome Blackie. Then little Gracie became ill. When we took her to the vet, the outcome wasn't one that we had anticipated. Gracie couldn't go home. Her heart was playing out and the kindest decision had to be made right then. We hated the decision that had to be made. We had five little boxes on my mantel where other "decisions" rested. I think her little heart broke when Duncan took off over the Rainbow Bridge.

Meanwhile back at the ranch, Blackie had decided, too. "I'm here. I'm making Stan get off the sofa and walk me. And besides, I've fallen in love with you guys and think you feel the same about me, at least I hope so."

> He loved to watch the squirrels
> outside Stan's window.

Well, big Blackie had nailed us right! Stan and I had a lesson waiting for us: rescue dogs cannot be adopted without neutering. Our Old Blackie had to face the knife at age nine—not a happy camper about that decision. After his close encounter with the knife, a personality quirk surfaced. Blackie now became very territorial, growling at dogs he passed on walks with Stan, as much as to say, "You got something I don't have anymore! Back off."

But he had Stan and vice versa and they were the greatest of buddies and known by all the neighbors—Stan the Man in his ever present black coat and hat with his pal Blackie to match. Stan bought a black Jeep that served to include Blackie in jaunts.

Then Stan became ill. Thirty days in ICU, followed by 15 more in Hospice. Blackie could visit at the latter and did every time invited. He loved to lick Stan's hands and talk to him with his big brown eyes. Blackie loved to watch the squirrels outside Stan's window robbing the birds' feeder while hanging upside down. He just watched quietly with never a move to interrupt. Blackie was too big and strong for me to walk him. I just weighed a few pounds more than he did! I hired neighbor kids to help. Then Adam, the grandson who adopted me and his parents, my "bonus daughter and son" built me a fence off the lower patio for Blackie so he could get out and run without me being dragged for the ride. Stan went to join Duncan and Gracie. Not too long after, Blackie joined them all. I became a true empty nester in a short period of time.

But, if there is one thing I've learned, it is this: into each life some rain must fall. And so much has fallen into mine! But don't you know, it takes rain to make rainbows which open the heart to beautiful memories.

I must share a humorous story about Mr. Blackie at this point. He became so very protective of me when we lost Stan, that I feared he might injure visitors and workers. I'd frequently put him on the

179

back deck where he was out of reach. After hauling garden hoses around my third of an acre for 20 years, I decided it was time for a sprinkler system. I found a crew after completing my due diligence scoping pros and recommendations and lots of interviewing. When they arrived, I put Blackie on the deck that also served as the roof to the lower walkout patio. While the crew was digging trenches in the lawn, the manager went to the back lower patio to check the water outlet located there. He came dashing up the stairs, mopping his head with a kerchief.

"What's the matter, Frank?" I asked.

"Your dog peed on my head!" he answered.

"Oh, my goodness! Jump into a shower. They all have shampoo!"

"Yeah, J C, BUT they don't have any water!

We turned it off to install the sprinklers!"

I gave him a watering can and a package of wet wipes and offered to ask a neighbor if he could use their facilities, which he refused. His home was some miles away and his whole crew was at the ready. What was a man to do at a time like that?!

I've always heard a good belly laugh can gain you five more years of life. If that's true, I'll never die! Every time I tell the story, I can't help laughing like a fool—along with those I share the story. And to this day, I believe that Blackie decided that Frank was in the wrong place. This was his space and nobody else but me belonged.

Food for Thought ...

I like you 'cuz I like me when I'm with you!

20

Meet J C at Home
Sweet Home

1998

*It didn't take me long to convince Stan that we had
a true diamond in the rough.*

I'VE ENJOYED A magnificent life, circling the
globe four times, and living eleven years abroad—
Germany twice: Bangkok, Thailand, and Okinawa—
not to mention the times that I traveled through
Europe with my girlfriends. I've retired from the
Pentagon and kissed a lot of "45's"—45 years in
real estate; 45 years of golfing; and 45 years skiing
the slopes I loved so well throughout the world. I'm
looking forward to what I can rack up and declare
what I've done 90 times! By that birthday, my first

book—the one you are reading—will have been published ... who knows what it will have done to stir my imagination and the imagination of others to get the juices flowing for bigger and better things. Definitely, it's another PLUS! Will it be a cruise of the Greek Isles or renting a house on Santorini and including all my besties to join me?

FORTY FIVE YEARS came into play once again! Angie's List on the internet just brought to my attention that that my home is 45 years old and must need some things done. Indeed, it does! But Stan and I got a whale of a bargain at $150,000! The home has now been assessed by the Douglas County Assessor's office to be in excess of $500,000.

Oh yes, there were expenses to offset our increased value. First, we had to pay the overdue taxes of the prior owners before we could even take possession of what was to be our "forever" home.

The soon to be previous owners were about to lose it for unpaid taxes. Knowing that the tax man was looming, we didn't know what we could have picked it up for that way. Surely, there was someone else out there who might be sniffing around and could see the hidden beauty that we saw. And surely, that someone would attempt to ace us out before we could get our bid in ... if merely to have the sensational view and extra space between homes. We didn't want to take any chances in losing it.

For nine years, the owners had left it vacant when they decided to relocate to North Carolina. Their son checked on it now and again during that time, but no one made it a home—or wanted to—'til we saw the potential. I was staying with my friends, Arlene and Dean Zick, who invited me to share their home in Parker. Their three kids had left for college or marriage and they had room to spare, so I nestled in a suite on the lower level of their home.

Arlene and I had been roomies in 1960 and traveled Europe in 1962. Arlene had become a gourmet cook and Dean a gourmand. I was lucky enough to be both! She never cooked when four of us gals shared an apartment. We ate very well!

This was not a pièce de résistance!

When the owner of 6834 called me to ask for value quote on his home, I was forced to ask for a time out 'til my car became less of a snowy marshmallow and the Zick's driveway allowed me to exit. No one could go anywhere for the same reason: we were all stuck ... it was the Blizzard of October 1997.

When the snow abated, we were finally able to meet at his house. He had scheduled the trip from North Carolina to move the remainder of furniture and objects they'd left nine years before and rent or sell the house. I rang his doorbell.

Like most homeowners, he wanted to know what monetary rewards he could anticipate when his home sold. After sitting vacant lo those many years it needed A LOT ... and I mean A LOT of maintenance and attention! The main décor was dull and gruesome ... the early 70s browns, greens, golds even to all the kitchen appliances, linoleum on kitchen floor, plus a barfy brown, gold, and green shag carpet in family room. There were single pain windows and three sets of sliders. I still wonder to this day how the empty cereal boxes got there. We discovered dead birds in the main floor fireplace and the walkout basement was unfinished. You get the picture? This was not a pièce de résistance!

I was enthralled by the magnificent mountain views!!

I did some serious calculating; considered all improvements necessary to be able to rent the place; determined the max listing price if improvements were made; and compared it to like houses selling at that time in the neighborhood. I offered to put him in touch with qualified professionals who could provide the needed fixes.

His visit was too short to allow for overseeing of necessary improvements, nor did he know who to hire. He didn't have the skills or aptitude to do improvements himself and just wanted to get on with it and leave the anticipated headaches behind him. North Carolina was beckoning to him to return quickly; he wanted to get back to his wife and life.

He revealed that he'd offered it to the mover he'd hired to take the rest of their things to the East Coast. The price was reasonable, considering all the work that needed to be done. That is, if his "mover" buyer could obtain mortgage approval and if the buyer could do much of the work himself, but that wasn't going to happen.

I strolled along the 30 foot deck that stretched from the family room to the master suite. I was enthralled by the magnificent mountain views! Sadly, it has since been compromised by the growth of neighbors' fir trees—bound to happen—but I still have wonderful views from some portions of the deck. I thought the price quoted to the mover was a steal. Hmmm ... maybe, just maybe, this would be the perfect home for Stan the Man and yours truly.

Stan decided he was going to relocate to Colorado when he retired. We agreed to buy it at the price quoted to the mover. It didn't take me long to convince Stan that we had a true diamond in the rough. That it was a worthy investment and with the help of many friends, it was the gem we were looking for. His skills, though artistic, did not include reconstruction. No matter—his savings answered that problem, providing for materials and professional laborers.

Our dear friends rolled up their sleeves and went to work on the many tasks they knew how to do. I will ALWAYS be so grateful to them! The baseboard gas hot water heat along the floors was a winner—the question was: how to cool during the summer? We installed ceiling fans throughout and later added an evaporated cooler to the roof. New counters and sink replaced the old and hardwood floors were done throughout, including the colorful, very dated, not to mention, dreaded linoleum.

The harvest gold refrigerator waltzed out the front door and was replaced with the latest in stainless. We got a secondhand freezer chest purchased from a client who was moving for the price of a case of his favorite beer—such a deal! And still working 30 years later! He even moved it from his house to our garage. Finally, all the windows and sliders were replaced—goodbye single pane windows—definitely not preferred in Colorado.

My cousin Betty and her year old Sheltie, Duncan were staying with me while her apartment was being shown to potential buyers. Betty and I were the last of our families, best friends and legal advocates for each other since we could remember. Her roommate of 40 years had just died of cancer. One of the major reasons for my return to Colorado was Betty's impending loss and need for my compassion.

We decided that she could take up residence in the guest room when her condo sold. I was in the kitchen, creating a pie, when she came out of her room, struggling to breathe. Less than two blocks from the house is a fire station. Emergency vehicles from there plus another fire station team responded immediately to my call in minutes. They both worked on Betty; then determined they needed to get her to emergency STAT ... meaning the closest hospital. Since that date in 1998, three hospitals have been built within a 10 minute ride. The ONLY one at that moment was Swedish—a good 45 minutes away.

Betty was loaded up and off they went. I followed in my car as no one could ride with the patient unless there was return transportation. When I entered Swedish Emergency, and asked for my cousin, I received an unconscionable reply from a male nurse who was leading me to her. "You know, of course, that she died enroute?"

That created an immediate problem.

Just how the hell would I have known THAT?!
They almost had a second patient by the time I
reached Betty. She still was intubated—a shocking
sight in itself, and I really had to call on my Best
Friend, God, at this point to see me through this
shocking situation! Before I knew it, I was greeted
by a minister who was on call in the hospital. He
was there for both moral support and assistance
in completion of a variety of forms.

Before Betty had moved in with me, she and I had
talked about donor considerations if either of us
were in an accident. We both wanted to help others
if our time was up and to help those in need of
organs. That created an immediate problem. I knew
that Betty had had breast cancer. A huge question
surfaced: did she have chemo or radiation?

Time was of the essence. ... How was I to find out?
It was after midnight. I drove like I was in a race
car to her apartment and searched through all the

papers I could find. I had no idea who to call for the answer. Who would know?

Without getting a solution, the hospital advised me that the only donation that wouldn't be exempt would be her corneas. Where do I sign? Someone today is observing a beautiful world—thanks to my dear cousin Betty! I only wish that I'd been privy to her medical treatment. The information may have helped more people in need.

Food for Thought ...

Lesson to others ... be an organ donor ... and let others know that is your wish. If you have had chemo or radiation, it's a good thing to let those who will make decisions on your behalf know.

21

Children of My Heart

Their uniqueness and love have become pieces in my quilt of life, creating a kaleidoscope of colors and weaves in new fabrics that I never envisioned could be possible.

THE MOST DISAPPOINTING thing in my life was to learn I couldn't have children. I loved kids and wanted so much to be a mother. It tightens my jaws when I witness children being abused, abandoned, and even murdered by a parent. Why God? Why wasn't that child given to me?

So, I'm not going to be a mom ... it wasn't to be. Then, I'd do it my way.

I adopted my children in my heart and at every opportunity I could.

There's so much to tell about each of "my kids" ... do you have a few hours?

Meet my "daughter" Yvonn.

Yvonn Habermann ... between flights for Lufthansa.

The last time I lived in Germany, I shared with you that I had painted a Santa on my large glass storm door. Neighbors walking children would routinely stop to inquire about him. Where did I get him? How could they get one? When I revealed that I had created him, they wanted to know if I would make one for them.

Of course, I would, and they got a Santa on their door. What I got was new, lifelong friends. Yvonn was seven at the time she first fell in love with my door Santa. When she graduated from her German high school at 17, her mom asked if I'd take her into my home in America for three months so she could acquire American English. Three months expanded to a full year. Yvonn graduated from my alma mater and is still in my life.

Today, she's a flight attendant for Lufthansa. When she can't pop in for a visit in person, we tech communicate multiple times per week. Today at 50, she embraces the life of a world traveler.

Meet my "daughter" Vanina.

Vanina came from France for a few months and stayed
for over a year—loved having her with me.

I always light up when I hear the French lilt of her
voice over the phone. She lived with me for over a
year when the family she had been with expanded
and no longer had room for an "extra."

She became a lovely daughter who walked and
took care of my pair of Shelties while I worked
and traveled. Eventually, she returned to France;
married and had a son and daughter.

Meet Jennifer and Jonathan who "adopted" me!

Granddaughters Madi in pink and Hannah in blue
in their Princess tent!

We met at a South Metro Realtor Association
meeting and instantly connected. Both their mothers
had died, and both instantly felt that I would be the
perfect Mom for them. They gave me a bonus: they
gifted me with two of the dearest granddaughters,
Madi and Hannah Rose. And Madi, she introduced
me to *Star Wars* ... as in using the *Star Wars* theme
at her wedding. Both are beautiful, smart, and
each graduating with high honors: one from the

University of Denver and the other from Denver High School a week later. I love it when I get to participate in their graduations and ongoing celebrations.

Celebrating Jennifer's 50th birthday with Hanna.

Meet my "Grandson" Adam.

Adam's mom helped me clear my storage room, bringing Adam along to help. Between the three of us, we filled several carloads of boxes and bags and off we went to the Salvation Army to deliver our bounty.

His Gramma had died some time ago. He asked his mom if it would be all right to adopt me as his Gramma. "Well, ask her," was her reply. He did.

My answer, "In a New York nanosecond!" Not only did I gain a wonderful grandson, but dear friends: his mom Nancy as a daughter and Dad Scott as a son—an entire extended family! Can't get any better!

Meet my newest "son" Ethan.

A recent high school graduate and ultimate lawn mower! Not only best mower in Pinery, Colorado, but the sweetest most polite young man. One Christmas, my elderly adopted Aussies were kicking up a fuss at the living room window. Going to see what the matter was, I found Ethan out front putting up his own Christmas lights on the front of my home so I could enjoy them—complete with timer. He wanted to surprise me ... but the dogs beat him to it. Yet, surprised I was and delighted beyond words. My Man Stan was always the light hanger. Since he had died, I had no one to do the task ... that was until Ethan came into my life. What a thoughtful, compassionate young man!

There's so much to tell about each of "my kids" ... do you have a few hours? I'm a very proud Mom and Gramma! Each came into my life unexpectantly, but most welcomed and remained and some multiplied. God knew we needed each other. Their uniqueness and love have become pieces in my quilt of life, creating a kaleidoscope of colors and weaves in new fabrics that I never envisioned could be possible. It truly makes my life glorious and full!

Mom and Pop had enough love to adopt an orphanage, but only birthed this one lucky chick. They taught me by observation, how to form the extended outreach family. They had apartments they rented to young military couples stationed at Fort Riley, who became the kids they couldn't have. There are many of their offspring named after Mom and Pop and even after me, who most never knew. Each has made my life richer.

Food for Thought ...

Friends and relatives are the gifts we give ourselves.

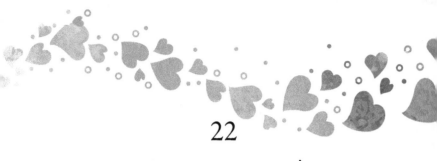

22

Don't Get Stuck
on "Someday Isle"

2020 Looking at Yesteryear

*I've learned: out of everything bad,
there is something good!*

THERE'S A PLACE in your imagination called
"Someday Isle"—a castle of dreams, surrounded
by a moat full of alligators of doubt and ready to
destroy dreams as they occur. All have the same first
name only: "Someday" as in, my name is Someday
I'll learn a craft ... Someday I'll change careers ...
Someday I'll travel to the moon—something my
father was certain of happening in his lifetime.

The next postcard would be from there on my wildest exploration. I think I inherited my love of wanderlust from Mom, who would go anywhere at the drop of a hat. Whether it was to check out a new restaurant or movie or play or a trip. She was pretty much stuck in Junction City, where they were both born, so the later was a highlight in her life. Her dream of travel was to come.

I took extra jobs to bring them to Europe while I lived there. Mom was excited about seeing Germany, where her mother was born, but alas and alak, Pop would not travel out of sight of his fishing hole. Said he'd left nothing there he had to go back for. We could have visited England together from whence Great Grandfather York brought the seed that finally made my father a York and Scotland and introduced Grandma York's Scottish ancestry.

Though opportunity was there for both and Mom did yearn to travel, it was Pop that pulled down the damper. His emotional alligators, far bigger than Mom could even imagine, had devoured the opening. Mom would not go without Pop! They both forfeited a grand adventure.

The travel window opened once again for my parents.

One Christmas, I flew home from Bangkok for Mom's pending surgery and planned a stopover in Portland, Oregon where Uncle Logan's Union Pacific Railroad career had moved his family years before. Mom and her sister/best friend visited each other annually, one year in Kansas—next Oregon. Pop would never go further than Rawlins, Wyoming, a time or two to visit his sister Naomi.

When the money I'd saved for their venture was refused, I got a movie camera and took pictures of

everywhere I went from then on. When I went
home to visit, I'd take reels of films. We'd throw
a sheet over the clothesline; pop the corn; cut the
watermelon and call all the relatives and neighbors
to grab their lawn chairs and join us. Pop got such a
thrill out of traveling "his" way. His fave film—one
of the Thunderbirds flying in formation at an air
show he could watch for hours.

The travel window opened once again for my
parents. Mom was scheduled to have surgery.
In my most convincing voice, I convinced them
both to accept the sleeper train tickets I'd bought
them and to meet me in Portland for Christmas
before she had it. Pop relented with pushes from
both Mom and me—at least we weren't insisting on
a plane trip, which was his emotional tipping point.
He would never know the pleasure I found in my
trips abroad. When we arrived on the West Coast,
definitely a far cry from Kansas, Pop finally saw

an ocean for the first time. He was thrilled at the vastness as compared to his hometown fishin' hole.

My three cousins in Portland were the brothers and sister I'd never had. I always stopped off there when possible and for many years after returning home, attended their annual family campouts in Washington and Oregon. My cousins' kids thought I was their Auntie Mame and wanted me to adopt them if anything, God forbid, happened to their parents! Of course, I would! They loved my stories of ventures from the around the world and thought it would be super neat to jump into my suitcase and share my travels.

We returned to Kansas and proclaimed it to be the most wonderful Christmas in all our lives. I gave up flying back to join Mom and Pop on the train. I thought we'd NEVER get to Kansas. It took three days instead of two hours! One afternoon,

I walked through the club car and met an old friend that I last saw in Europe. We instantly reconnected and talked, laughed and ate our way to Kansas for the remainder of the trip.

I've learned: out of everything bad, there is something good! While I was having a pleasant time with lots of reminiscing with Lynne, my folks found the books I'd bought them on the trails we were crossing over most interesting. Pop sketched scenery and people to pass the time. They were happy: I was happy.

As soon as we hit home, we made it to the doctor to see if Mom and her doctor were ready for the surgery. Pop had started having some health issues enroute back that put him in the hospital for a surgery as well. With them both in the hospital, all I could think was *Thank you, God, for bringing me home this particular time.*

The joys we had had in Oregon were now overridden with anxiety. I extended my stay with Mom and Pop 'til I was sure they'd be all right. Pop's sister Naomi came from Wyoming to help them. A month passed and the doctor and Naomi assured me all was well enough for me to return to Thailand and my job with Dillingham, Zachary, Kaiser. I could help them better financially by returning. There were no jobs available in JC.

Pop stayed home and tended his fishing hole. Not so Mom—she had the travel bug. When she heard that I had a conference I needed to attend in Hawaii, Mom and her sister Louise booked their flights and hotel at the same time. Now travel became something she looked forward to.

Food for Thought ...

"Someday Isle" is an imaginative place in your heart and mind. Don't get stuck on it with too many doubts and maybes. If there's something you want to see or do so—go for it! Find a way! Don't go to your grave with your music still inside you! It's not a time for regrets and I wish I had. Play it on your heartstrings—loudly enough for all to hear!

23

Living Well Is the Best Reward

*I was driving myself crazy with all the
fractures in my life.*

I WAS BORN IN the worst of times. My family
and extended family struggled through the Great
Depression ... through the hate and destruction
of World War II ... from losing friends to dreaded
diseases like polio and the rage of cancer ... the wrath
of smoking that all thought was so cool, and healthy,
turned out to be a ticket to illness and death for many.
Then came the time it wasn't smart if you did smoke.
As one of my German friends said, "We get too late
smart ... and too soon old."

Life ...

Life sent me two husbands: one who broke my heart ... the other who broke my finances. I was exonerated by the church from the one who broke my heart as he took off to dry his kid's diapers in my Christmas gift dryer. I swore I would never marry again. Yet eight years later, I ate my words when I was wooed by a Texan while working in Germany who I romantically married in Thailand. Years later, he robbed my company and nearly destroyed me financially with his deceptions and lies.

My heart was stepped on many times by unfaithful friends, suitors and mates. One couple covered for the husband who squandered my savings and company claiming that my success had made him feel inadequate. Therefore, he was justified in doing what he did.

I adored my mother and forewarned her not to get in the car with her brother as the driver ... a drinking driver. One day, he convinced her to take a drive, bringing their poodles. Stopping off at Uncle Lee's old buddy's locker plant a few miles from their home, Lee drove under an 18-wheeler carrying kitchen cabinets. The result was a blazing inferno. My dear mom and uncle never knew what happened.

In my distress, I spent days wandering the farms and fields, searching for the last bit of life from that tragic scene, asking everyone I could contact if she or he seen a little apricot poodle. I was driving myself crazy with all the fractures in my life.

No one is exempt.

The greatest threat to the world since my birth is in rocket speed as I wrote these final chapters. Coronavirus has struck everyone ... everywhere!

My "adopted heart" daughter Yvonn, who flies Lufthansa as a flight attendant, texted that Panama is closed. She was on her way to Bangkok. I watched news from Bangkok that said COVID-19 was making itself known in Thailand.

It has entered every country ... a global pandemic. Previously happy travelers return from ships and planes—many dying in overcrowded hospitals where nurses and physicians are exhausted. No one is exempt—from a tiny baby to senior citizens. Medical supplies and testing is sorely lacking. Churches and schools are closed. Grocery stores are depleted with aisles of empty shelves. Restaurants and parks are closed. Millions have been furloughed or lost their jobs. It's nothing like what I can remember from the Great Depression days ... it's not just a shortage of toilet paper ... it feels like a modern day Armageddon. I am bewildered and lacking an answer.

Life is filled with obstacles and challenges. I know this; I've experienced it. It's not just recognizing those stumbling stones along the way. It's turning them into stepping-stones—a means of progress or advancement—to rise above the seemingly impossible.

In my heart, I know we will survive! And learn—as always—from painful experiences. I pray your faith and courage will see you through this and open opportunities to decide: what are you doing the rest of your life? An excellent question ... what's your answer?

Food for Thought ...

It always seems darker before the dawn. But the sun continues to rise. Keep your faith!

24

My Final Thoughts

The greatest reward is to live a life well.

I ALWAYS KNEW I would have hearts on the cover of my book and sprinkled throughout. Love ... is the rarest and dearest of gifts. Please, remember to share it with everyone.

To LOVE yourself. If you don't, how can you expect others to?

LOVE wasn't put in your heart to stay ... LOVE isn't love until you give it away.

The kind of self-love of which I write, and speak, is not narcissistic and selfish. It's self-appreciation, never self-deprecation. Once you feel it coming from within, plant the seed in all you pass each day. Give everyone a smile from the heart. Something that is so easy-to-plant seeds, and so rewarding to watch grow.

The one who needs love most, is the one who peppers the world with hate ... on others and on actions of lives trying to do good things.

Even nature's critters respond to love. Try feeding the wild birds each morning. They give back ten-fold with their singing and beauty. Feed the hungry. Help dress the poor. And share your wisdom. Help educate those who haven't had the opportunity to learn new skills—from reading to writing and beyond. Most are surprisingly quick learners. Rejoice in how everyone can make a difference.

An old friend of mine who knew her time was about up, was being interviewed by the deacon of her church about her wishes for her final day on earth. He asked her about the friends she'd like to have present; what music she'd like played/sung and by whom; the readings she'd like to share; what kind of reception should follow; what memorials should be suggested; plus anything she especially desired.

Her answers:

If it's inconvenient, folks shouldn't feel the need to come to say goodbye. I'll await their hello later. We've all shared happy times better remembered. If they have some extra change in their pockets, share with those in need—the homeless, hungry, or ill. They'll know who they are. Or consider Cancer League of Colorado, an all-volunteer group with 100% of proceeds going to fund the cures for cancer or Alzheimer's, with no cure yet found to date. Both have robbed us of the ones we love in one way or another. If they love God's creatures, shelter animals. Wildlife and birds need food, refuge and love and will return your love 100 fold. The choice is theirs and certainly nothing is expected. Just pay the love they've given me forward and find a common seed to feed their friendships. Thank you for the honor and pleasure of being my friend.

As the deacon was about to leave, she added,

Oh yes, there's one more thing. Please put a fork in my hand.

The deacon looked puzzled.

You know after church suppers, someone comes around to collect the plates. The person says, 'Please keep your fork. Something really good is coming next.'

Looking back as I enter my 88th year, I've had a rich life. Of course, there are some parts I would have liked to have bypassed. But they are parts that have contributed to who I am. My original intention in writing *What Are You Doing the Rest of Your Life?* was to share my personal depths of despair and how I overcame them. I intended to encourage you to seek for yourself the way over, under or through the blockage and succeed. And, I wanted to share the amazing the fun and surprises I've had along the way.

WowZee ... whatta ride I have had ... and there's more to come! Someday, I will meet the end. A full life that is exonerated! Yes, the greatest reward is to live a life well.

Life is not a journey to the grave—
with the intention of arriving safely in a pretty
and well-preserved body, but rather, skidding
in broadside, thoroughly worn out—
with—chocolate strawberries in one
hand—and stem of red in the other—
and loudly proclaiming:

WOWZEE!
WHATTA RIDE!

Make sure that your life is a WowZee one, too!

In Gratitude

My book would never have happened without these people in my life. Appearing at the right time, and certainly, in the right place,

DR. JUDITH BRILES, The Book Shepherd. With the patience of JOB and the wisdom of SOCRATES, Dr. Judith Briles, The Book Shepherd and Coach Supreme, guided me through the pillars of writing/publishing knowledge to completion of my FIRST BOOK. A long-standing dream and desire of a lifetime. And now, REALIZED! Thank you, Dear Judith, for sharing your keen knowledge and precious time with this novice. I could NOT have done it without YOU!

NICK ZELINGER, Book cover designer and artistic creator. Many thanks, Nick, for turning my love of hearts and my life logo into such a beautiful invitation to my readers to open the book. The rainbow hearts and reflections dance around the cover and throughout the book invite love into the stories of my life happenings.

MICHELLE RENEE, Website builder and designer. Thank you for giving the reader a peek into my life and encouraging them to add life and zest to their lives in their decisions of "What Are They Doing the Rest of Their Lives."

CONNIE PSHIGODA came into my life via Parker Newcomers. In hosting a book celebration event in honor of her book, *The Wise Woman's Almanac*, in my home, I revealed that I was interested in publishing a book that has always been in my heart. I asked, "Who would she recommend I talk to?"

"There's only one person—Judith Briles." I called her and the finished book is in your hands.

MARGIE WARNER, whose words to me in first grade when I told her I wanted to write a book someday—imagine a 6 year old claiming such!—was that I couldn't. Yes, I could ... your words became a driver for me to accomplish just about anything forward when I was told by others that I couldn't do something.

COUSIN ROSEMARIE and **HUSBAND DUKE,** every Easter and Thanksgiving have been a pure joy to spend with you. Thank you.

You've all been most patient with this novice writer and have helped me immeasurably to make my dream a reality! THANK YOU from the bottom of my HEART!

Jeanene  Childers

About J C Childers

CURIOUS AND LIFE-LONG learner would be two areas that J C Childers excels in ... along with being a heart mom, dog mom, Toastmaster speaker, Mahjong player, golfer, skier, global traveler, swimmer, certified chocoholic, red wine sipper, art dabbler, and a believer in the *why not*. And, oh yes, life-long friend to countless women, men and children around the world.

As J C approaches her 10th decade of living as an embracer of life, she is a believer in sharing ... as in sharing what she has done; looking at a problem—any problem—and figuring out how to solve it or overcome it and still keep one's sanity. After all, she believes if life deals you a lemon ... grab the vodka and call the girls!

Her travels, some solo, many with *the girls*, even in her beloved Model T Ford that she sold during her 8th decade was a steady ride. All have taken her to more places than most would ever dream of venturing to. The riches in adventures and memories could take her to the Moon, circle it 100 times, then return to Earth. Her home is a treasure chest of memories, travels, artifacts, even a bar that she hauled back from Bangkok!

J C is about living. About friendship. About sharing. About caring. And most of all, about the love of life.

Of course, her memoir—her book—would be called *What Are You Doing the Rest of Your Life?* She knows what she's planning on doing ... do you?

www.JCChildersAuthor.com

Working with J C Childers

Bring J C to Your Group or Book Club

Every group has some type of gathering. Whether a live, in-person event or one that needs to reach to remote sites of the world, J C has the energy and the wisdom to connect, delight, and set the stage for your event or meeting. With humor and a "you can do it attitude," she will be the perfect kickoff, luncheon or wrap-it-up speaker.

What Are You Doing the Rest of Your Life?

Bring Some Fun and Energy and Life's Perspective from a woman who's been around the world four different times and embraces each day from the moment she gets up to the last drop of "the red" when she goes to bed.

Around the World With J C

In J C's 88 Years, she has crisscrossed the globe meeting new friends, discovering amazing cultures, and adopting new Heart Children. Starting from Junction City, Kansas, to Thailand, to Okinawa, to France, to Italy, to Africa, to Australia, to New Zealand, and maybe to your city! She's ready to share some adventures with you.

Children of the Heart

J C has her "adopted" Heart Children from all parts of the world—a total of seven! The richness of the fabric of multiple cultures has woven a kaleidoscope of beauty and memories for her and for them.

To bring J C to your event, contact her at:

www.JCChildersAuthor.com
JCRealt@outlook.com
303-475-3015

Next from J C Childers ...

PAWS and SMILE

Every one of us who have had "Fur Children" to love has reached a time with our little four legged friends—a time where difficult decisions must be made. The vet has proclaimed them suffering and in need of a peaceful release into the hands of God. We know it's one of the hardest—tho kindness— decisions we can make.

They've completed their job here on earth, and they're ready for the next step, introducing themselves to God. He loves these little creatures, too.

I know, you wish you could keep each one of them in your life forever, but God's plan was greater. There were many little fur fellows just waiting for their turn in your heart. They've entertained you and left you with fond memories as well as some really funny stories.

Allow me to share some of those stories with you in my forthcoming audio book *PAWS and SMILE*. Watch for it on Amazon.

THANK YOU FOR JOINING ME ON MY JOURNEY.

NOW, IT'S YOUR TURN!

What are you doing the rest of *your* life? What plans have you created to change your dreams, your wishes, into a reality? When will you start?

Make a list of the 10 or more things you've always wanted to do; why you haven't; and when you will. Check 'em off and date 'em as you do 'em. You can do anything you set your mind to. Surprise yourself!

MY BUCKET LIST

What I want MOST   **WHEN I'll do it**

_____   _____

_____   _____

_____   _____

_____   _____

MY BUCKET LIST

What I want MOST   **WHEN I'll do it**

_____   _____

_____   _____

_____   _____

_____   _____

_____   _____

_____   _____

_____   _____

_____   _____

_____   _____

_____   _____

MY BUCKET LIST

What I want MOST **WHEN I'll do it**

_____   _____

_____   _____

_____   _____

_____   _____

_____   _____

_____   _____

_____   _____

_____   _____

_____   _____

_____   _____

_____   _____

Love is a present that special people give...
It brings a touch of beauty to every day they live.

CPSIA information can be obtained
at www.ICGtesting.com
Printed in the USA
FSHW021958260721
83581FS